P9-CRT-150

CRAFT CHALLENGE

DOZENS OF WAYS TO REPURPOSE A

pILLoWCASE

DOZENS OF WAYS TO REPURPOSE A
PILLOWCASE

Suzanne J.E. Tourtillott

LARK BOOKS
A Division of Sterling Publishing Co., Inc.
New York / London

Library of Congress Cataloging-in-Publication Data

Tourtillott, Suzanne J. E.
   Craft challenge : dozens of ways to repurpose a pillowcase / Suzanne J.E.
Tourtillott. -- 1st ed.
      p. cm.
   Includes index.
   ISBN 978-1-60059-402-1 (pb-trade pbk. : alk. paper)
   1. Needlework. 2. Handicraft. I. Title.
   TT752.T69 2009
   746.4--dc22

                                          2008038952

10 9 8 7 6 5 4 3 2 1

First Edition

Published by Lark Books, A Division
of Sterling Publishing Co., Inc.
387 Park Avenue South, New York, NY 10016

© 2009, Lark Books

Distributed in Canada by Sterling Publishing,
c/o Canadian Manda Group, 165 Dufferin Street
Toronto, Ontario, Canada M6K 3H6

Distributed in the United Kingdom by GMC Distribution Services,
Castle Place, 166 High Street, Lewes, East Sussex, England BN7 1XU

Distributed in Australia by Capricorn Link (Australia) Pty Ltd.,
P.O. Box 704, Windsor, NSW 2756 Australia

The written instructions, photographs, designs, patterns, and projects in this volume are in-
tended for the personal use of the reader and may be reproduced for that purpose only.
Any other use, especially commercial use, is forbidden under law without written permission
of the copyright holder.

Every effort has been made to ensure that all the information in this book is accurate.
However, due to differing conditions, tools, and individual skills, the publisher cannot be
responsible for any injuries, losses, and other damages that may result from the use of the
information in this book.

If you have questions or comments about this book, please contact:
Lark Books
67 Broadway
Asheville, NC 28801
828-253-0467

Manufactured in China

All rights reserved

ISBN 13: 978-1-60059-402-1

For information about custom editions, special sales, premium and corporate
purchases, please contact Sterling Special Sales Department at 800-805-5489 or
specialsales@sterlingpub.com.

Senior Editors
Nicole McConville and Kathy Sheldon

Assistant Editor
Beth Sweet

Art Director
Dana Irwin

Art Production
Carol Morse

Illustrator
Orrin Lundgren

Photographer
Lynne Harty

Cover Designer
Amy Sly

*This book is dedicated to the clever crafter-sewers everywhere
who live to plunder linens.*

contents

Live

Re-crafting the pillowcase

WHEN IS A PILLOWCASE NOT A PILLOWCASE? When you, crafty sewer, take the craft challenge and turn it into an amazing and inventive something else—a sweet little tunic, a bold pair of wrist cuffs, or a super-mod lampshade. You may already know that innovative crafting challenges have taken the blogging community by storm. These clever sewer-crafters find that transforming new or vintage pillowcase yard goods is both simple and satisfying. They post photos of finished pieces online for others to see and comment on.

Not all that savvy (yet) about online crafting? No problem—simply challenge yourself, or a sewing-circle of friends, to refashion the humble pillowcase into one of the dozens of projects included in this book. Either way, the fun is in the hunt for cases, the transformation process, and the sharing of results.

You'll discover that pillowcases are the newest and hottest of crafting canvases. Raid your closet (or your own bed!), scour the flea market, or even pillage a favorite department store for great pillowcases you can transform into something fabulous and entirely new. With their fresh prints, charming embroidery, and decorative hem ends, these affordable, versatile fabrics are just waiting to be discovered (by you!) and given their moment in the retro-chic sun.

Craft Challenge: Dozens of Ways to Repurpose a Pillowcase is the first in Lark's new re-crafting series. Here you'll see how some of the best designers took the pillowcase challenge and came up with stylish and often surprising results: fashionable clothing, haute home accessories, and gifts divine. Some projects really celebrate the unique aspects of pillowcase anatomy, whether yummy trims and embroidered details (like the Layer Cake Apron) or unabashedly feminine prints that make nostalgia look hip (try the Lavender Tote). Some will really make you wonder where the pillowcase is (or was). Their transformations are profound—who knew you could make a chic fabric bowl from bed linens?

If your sewing skills have been languishing in the back of the closet, take the informative guided tour through the Pillowcase Basics where you'll find a primer on tools and materials. Looking for ideas for embellishments? Need a reminder on how to do a French knot? They're here. You'll find a handy conversion chart to translate standard pillowcase sizes into fabric yardage and a sprinkling of little tips and suggestions that might give even seasoned sewers additional back-pocket skills.

So go, pillowcase explorers: repurpose those contemporary prints and fancy vintage cases. With your nimble fingers and our project ideas you can make pillowcases new and fresh—and find sewing more fun than it was ever, ever meant to be.

Looking for still more challenge in your crafting life? Find exclusive bonus projects, with inspiring photos, tips, and step-by-step instructions, at www.larkbooks.com/crafts.

pillowcase Basics

THE GOODS

half the fun of repurposing fabric is finding just the right diamond-in-the-rough, waiting to be transformed into something new. Where pillowcases are concerned, you're most likely to find yourself with a wonderful piece of cotton, whether it's the brightest of crisp whites or the most vibrant patterned fabric in rainbow hues.

Fortunately, cotton tends to be one of the easiest fabrics to care for. It's durable, washable, comfortable, and can be ironed and sewn with ease. Vintage pillowcases should be washed by hand. Prewash new cases according to the manufacturer's recommendations before use to make sure you get through any initial shrinking. Air-drying your completed pillowcase projects will ensure that your colors and handwork last for years to come.

VA-VA-VINTAGE

Most of our linen closets and attics have a few cherished pillowcase gems from years past. And if your search for vintage wonders comes up short, never fear. Just keep your eyes open at flea markets, antique shops, or online auctions for something that sparks your interest. Also remember that while many people have great linens stashed away, not everyone has the imagination of a clever crafter. Friends and acquaintances may jump at the chance to do a little closet purging while also helping fuel your creativity. From exquisite examples of hand-worked embellishments to brilliant floral and geometric prints of decades past, there's a treasure trove out there.

Even if what you have is stained or torn, chances are good that you can still use part of the fabric or decorative trim. In fact, some of these less than perfect items can be found for highly discounted prices. The only pillowcases to avoid are those in which the fibers themselves are damaged and suffer from severe neglect (i.e. mildew and rot). The best tactic is simply to feel the pillowcase. You can tell a lot by touching and manipulating the fabric. Does it feel durable? Thin or heavy? Stiff or soft? You'll be working with it and possibly wearing it, so it doesn't hurt to check out its tactile appeal.

EDGES DIVINE

One of the fun challenges of sewing a new piece from a pillowcase is trying to showcase the unique hem of the original article. That already-finished edge can become something functional, like a strap, or the inspiration for an entire decorative motif. And that's surely creative work: preserving a band of unique embroidery or rare lace while transforming all of the yard goods around it into something new, useful, or just plain beautiful.

Sewers have always treated the open end of the pillowcase as a kind of canvas, to show off elegant stitchery and cutwork. Some hems tell little stories or offer the words of a tune; others pay homage to traditional needlework, whether tatting, crochet, or lace. So use the lacy edge of a case as the hem of an apron or the brim of a hat. Let an embroidered edge take (bottom) center stage on a skirt.

Now, with stash in hand, you're ready to stock your sweet little sewing spot with the best tools and materials you can find. We show you the ins and outs of cutters, needles, facings, and more.

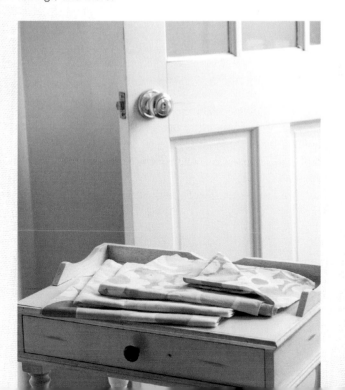

CASES TO YARD GOODS

If you've ever shopped at a thrift store, you know that a crafty shopper can find pillowcases in countless beautiful colors and patterns to suit nearly every taste, from modern to vintage. Better yet, all of these tastes are satisfied at a very affordable price. Now throw in the fact that cases come with pre-finished edges that are ideal for quick projects, and you can easily see that pillowcases are the ideal solution for the economical crafter.

Since sewing instructions usually list fabric yardage rather than "five king-size pillowcases," here's a handy chart.

DIMENSIONS		AREA*
20 x 30 inches (50.8 x 76.2 cm)	Standard	1 yard (0.8 m)
20 x 40 inches (50.8 x 101.6 cm)	King	1¼ yards (1.2 m)
12 x 16 inches (30.5 x 40.6 cm)	Baby	½ yard (0.5 m)
20 x 60 inches (50.8 x 152.4 cm)	Body	2¾ yards (2.5 m)
21 x 26 inches (53.3 x 66 cm)	Sham	¾ yd. (0.7 m)
26 x 26 inches (66 x 66 cm)	Euro	1½ yards (1.4 m)

*Area is based on a fabric width of 45 inches (114.3 cm).

THE NOTIONS

We have to admit that it's easy to get carried away with materials and tools. Once you've embraced this passion, your family may be eating off TV trays because you've taken over the dining room. But here's a secret you don't have to share: you need very little to make the projects in this book. If you're new to sewing, read on for practical advice about what to collect to get started.

Tip!

What's a raw edge? Thinking about uncooked food? You aren't far from the mark. A raw fabric edge has been cut but hasn't been finished with pinking shears or any type of stitching.

SEWING MACHINE

Forget the fancy machine. In fact, you could hand stitch every project in this book if desired. For the strongest seams and fastest results, however, there's nothing like using a sewing machine. A basic model will do: look for one that can make straight, satin, and zigzag stitches. If the project you want to make calls for a buttonhole, you'll also need that setting on your machine.

CUTTERS

You'll have a lot more fun sewing if you expand your collection to include more than just a pair of sharp scissors. These are a great starting point, of course, and you really need little more. Yet specialty cutting tools offer speed and precision you just can't get any other way.

Scissors

Two types are essential in every sewing kit: plain-old craft scissors (the kind you probably already have tucked away in a kitchen drawer) and dressmaker's shears that have sharp 8- to 10-inch (20.3 to 25.4 cm) blades and pointed tips. You can find the latter at any sewing supplies store. A good pair lasts a lifetime so it's worth investing in quality. Never (ever) use this fine pair for cutting paper! The wood fibers of paper dull blades quickly and render them useless on fabric.

Think about getting some appliqué scissors. One of the blades is wide and flat, which makes it easier to cut through a single piece of fabric in a stack.

Pinking Shears

The serrated edges of the blades on these specialty scissors cut tiny zigzags along fabric edges. This edge can be decorative, but the main purpose is to prevent the fabric from fraying.

Seam Ripper

Check the tool kit that came with your sewing machine: there's a good chance you already have one of these. A seam ripper is indispensable for a "reverse sewing," as many stitchers call ripping out stitching bloopers.

Rotary Cutter

Straight, long cuts are a breeze with this handy tool. Although not essential, the thick edge of a clear quilter's ruler is an excellent guide for rolling the cutter along the fabric. You must, however, always place a self-healing mat underneath the fabric before you start cutting. A rotary blade is sharp enough to destroy an unprotected surface but fragile enough to be easily damaged. When you find yourself pressing down on the cutter—or notice it skipping spots—it's time to replace the blade.

rotary cutter

Tip!
If a fabric is too delicate for pinking, place it on top of a sturdier fabric and then you can pink through both layers.

sewing machine

pinking shears

craft scissors

seam rippers

embroidery scissors

NEEDLES

Needles are cheap, so get quite a few and switch to a new one often. You probably won't notice that the needle you're using is ready for the trash until a dull point or a burr on the shaft snags a thread in your pillowcase fabric...and then you're stuck fixing the damage.

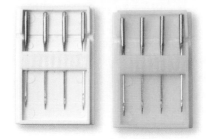

machine needles

Machine Needles

If you aren't too picky, for all of your stitching you can get away with a type and size of sewing machine needle called a universal 80/12. For delicate fabric, try switching to a finer needle—about a 60/8—and make sure that it's a type called a sharp.

Hand-Sewing Needles

Even experts have a tough time identifying most needle types by eyeballing them. The differences are subtle, but oh-so-important to stitch quality. Shorter betweens help quilters make small, even-length stitches. Sharps, which you'll use the most, are pointed to slip easily through woven fabric. Ballpoints are best for knits because they have rounded tips that push between fabric fibers, thus preventing snags.

hand-sewing needles

Embroidery Needles

The most common type is the crewel, which is short, has a sharp point, thin shaft, and large—but narrow—eye. Chenille needles, for yarn, are long and have sharp tips. Tapestry needles have dull tips that are suitable for weaving in yarn or thread ends and doing surface-only stitching (because the needle doesn't pierce the fabric and the dull tip won't split previously stitched floss). You don't need to know the numbering system or the types of needles; buy a package of assorted needles and experiment. You'll quickly gravitate to a favorite length, shaft thickness, and type of eye (round or slotted).

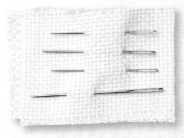

embroidery needles

Tip!

Want to start an argument? Ask a couple of stitchers the right way to insert pins through fabric layers: Some place pins along—or parallel to—seam lines, whereas others prefer a perpendicular placement.

ETC.

For whatever task you need to master—from marking fabric to making a seam—there's sure to be a tool or material that makes the job easier. Here, however, is a rundown of the notions that are most helpful.

Stitchers tend to accumulate notions at an amazing rate—and misplace them just as quickly. It's a good idea to get in the habit of storing everything in one place, preferably a portable container like the box on page 104.

the box on page 104.

straight pins

markers

needle threader

tape measure

TIP!

Use a pencil to mark lightly colored pillowcases, or use white chalk if your pillowcases are dark.

Straight Pins

All purpose (dressmaker's) pins are your best bet. Always remove pins as your fabric enters the stitching area on your sewing machine's bed. Hitting a pin can throw off the machine's timing, cause a snapped needle tip to bounce into your face, or dull the needle.

Loop, Point, and Corner Turners

The tip of your scissors will do in a pinch. To avoid damaging the fabric, however, a specialty notion is your best bet.

Markers

Water-soluble markers are an excellent alternative to chalk or transfer paper when you want to draw cutting, sewing, or design lines or marks on fabric. The disappearing inks can be quirky, though. Test your marker on a scrap of fabric to ensure that the lines eventually completely disappear. Also, remove the marks (either with water or with air-drying) before applying interfacing or a stabilizer—the chemicals in some products can make the marks permanent!

Needle Threader

Can't get those renegade threads through your needle? Use this little tool. Put the wire loop through the needle, insert the thread into the loop, pull back, and voilà!

Tape Measure

For accurate measuring along a curve, stand the tape measure on one of its edges.

trims

embroidery hoop

floss

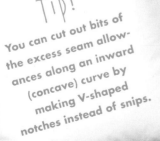

TIP!
You can cut out bits of the excess seam allowances along an inward (concave) curve by making V-shaped notches instead of snips.

sewing threads

Thread

Resist (indeed, boycott) the bargain bin of thread. Cheap thread is weaker and has barely visible slubs that prevent it from sliding easily through fabric and a machine needle's eye. It's best to match thread to the fabric content. In other words, use cotton or cotton-wrapped thread with cotton fabric and nylon or polyester thread with synthetic fabric.

Buttons

For a truly vintage touch, seek out older buttons at sewing shows and specialty shops. Or you can buy easy-to-use kits for covering buttons with the fabric of your choice. One of the best sources for old—and relatively new—buttons is charity-operated used clothing stores. Buy the dirt-cheap garments and cut off the buttons you want.

Floss

Each skein is a length of six loosely twisted strands of floss made from cotton, silk, or other fibers. Cut a length of floss no longer than about 20 inches (50.8 cm) and then pull the desired number of strands from one end.

Trims

More than a few of the projects in this book include the trim that already edges most pillowcases, so you don't have to worry about attaching your own lace or rickrack (unless you want to). See the techniques on page 27.

TIP!

Sometimes it's easier to add the trim before you sew the fabric pieces together, but most people prefer to attach it when their project is nearing completion so that they can fine-tune its position.

Iron and Ironing Board

Use what you have. If you want to get fancy, invest in a quality iron; it's heavier so that you get a better press faster. Craft and fabric shops sell mini-irons that get into tight spaces like corners. Work on any heat-safe surface or make your own ironing board cover (see page 122).

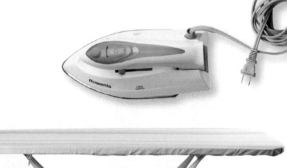

ironing board and iron

pillowcase MEMORY

My adult sister has had a security blanket her whole life—literally from birth to the present. Through the years, her blanket or "ienky" has gotten progressively more worn and torn. After mending and patching were no longer possible, my mom just threw it into a pillowcase, tied a knot at the end, and called it good. To this day, my sister still sleeps with her ienky—a worn, knotted pillowcase with a few measly blanket shreds inside.

Katy Hanson

INTERFACING

Areas of fabric that need a bit of strength can be reinforced on the underside with interfacing. This flat, plain material is sold in many weights (degrees of firmness). Choose one that's suitable for the type of fabric you're using. You also pick the interfacing by application: sew-in or fusible. The easiest type to use is fusible because it's attached to the entire back of the fabric with a glue-like resin that's activated by pressing with an iron. (Every project that calls for interfacing specifies what type to use.)

STABILIZERS

Permanent or temporary stabilizers help you sew on fabric that might pucker or act up in some other way. Sheets or strips can be basted, pressed, or sewn to the right side (front) or wrong side (underside) of a fabric. Starch and other types of liquid stabilizers can be sprayed or brushed on. After application, you sew the fabric. Then, depending on the type of stabilizer, you can pull it off, heat it with an iron until the stabilizer crumbles, or dip the fabric in water to dissolve it.

BATTING AND STUFFING

Not just for quilts! You could be using this puffy stuff (batting comes in lengths, stuffing is sold as a big bag of, well, fluff) for lining hot mitts (see page 112) or filling up a little beastie (see page 92). There are lots of types of batting and stuffing from cotton—which is rather flat and yields a folksy effect—to high-loft polyester, and even a type that's fusible on one side so that you can bond it to fabric. Unless a project calls for a specific type, choose whatever you fancy or the local store sells.

Don't Pin It on Me!

To avoid stepping on stray pins, keep a pincushion nearby when you cut and stitch —and always tuck your pins into it. You can have some fun by making your own (see page 124).

adhesive stabilizer

water-soluble stabilizer

tear-away stabilizer

light, medium, and heavyweight interfacing

pillowcase MEMORY

Halloween was always a time for extra creativity, and, when I was 12, my best friend and I decided to go all out on our costumes. It was important that we were a pair, so the costumes always had to be a set or a couple, or include both of us in some other way. That was the year we outdid ourselves! We sewed nightcaps and stocking caps and embroidered "His" and "Hers" on two softly faded family pillowcases. We cut holes for our arms and heads, pulled the cases over our heads, and went trick-or-treating as bed pillows. Our skinny little legs stuck out from under the cases, and we donned our best fuzzy slippers. We even used extra pillowcases for our treat sacks. So although they weren't the scariest of costumes, we were so proud of our handmade one-of-a-kind outfits!

Jacqueline Wolven

THE DETAILS

Once you have the necessary supplies to get started, it's time to take apart that pillowcase and re-assemble it into something really cool. You can avoid a drastic mistake by first reading through all of the steps in the project instructions. Before you know it, you'll be cutting away or using any of the other techniques described on the following pages. Begin all projects with a freshly pressed pillowcase, and keep in mind the sewing mantra "press as you go." (In other words, whenever you do something to the fabric, press it. This is especially important if the next step is topstitching.)

USING A PATTERN

A few of the projects call for a pattern. This is a simple shape that needs to be cut from the fabric. (You can see all of them starting on page 126). Just use a photocopier to enlarge the ones needed for your chosen project. Cut out these paper templates with your craft scissors and then switch to your shears to cut as many fabric shapes as you need.

MARKING AND TRANSFERRING ON FABRIC

Some of the patterns and all of the embroidery designs have lines or marks that need to be made on the fabric shapes. There are plenty of ways to do this, including using a light box, chalk, or transfer paper. The number one problem that stitchers encounter is ending up with a reverse image on the fabric. In other words, the lines and marks are on the left when they should be on the right, and vice versa.

HAND-SEWING STITCHES

It's true: you may have to do a bit of hand stitching to complete the project you like. We promise it won't be a lot. Of course, if you find hand stitching relaxing, go ahead and make all of your seams this way. Start by threading your needle and then secure the end with a knot or three tiny stitches in the same place in the fabric. Make three more tiny stitches at the end of the stitching before you cut off the excess thread.

Appliqué Stitch

Also called "hidden" or "invisible" stitch, it isn't meant to be seen when completed.

Basting Stitch

Very long straight stitches temporarily hold fabric layers together. Because basting stitches are long, they're easy to pull out after they've served their purpose. This stitch is the same as a running stitch, but with very long stitches that are easily removed after the permanent seam is in place.

Running Stitch

This stitch is created by weaving the needle through the fabric at evenly spaced intervals.

EMBROIDERY STITCHES

Start with a length of floss or very narrow silk ribbon—and don't knot the end. The best way to secure embroidery is to leave the last 1 or 2 inches (2.5 or 5.1 cm) on the underside and then lay this tail end across the back so that it's caught in the subsequent stitching.

Backstitch

A sturdier version of the straight stitch, the backstitch is good for stuffed projects, where seams are under pressure. Backstitches are also used to embroider decorative lines.

Blanket Stitch

The blanket stitch is a decorative and functional technique for accenting an edge or attaching a cut shape to a layer of fabric.

Cross Stitch

Fill an entire area with closely packed cross stitches, randomly scatter them across a surface, or use a single one to punctuate a design or represent an eye or nose.

French Knot

Don't hide this elegant knot! It goes on the surface of your piece to add depth and textural interest to the surface. It works well alone or grouped.

Satin Stitch

The satin stitch is composed of parallel rows of straight stitches and is often used to fill in an outline.

appliqué stitch

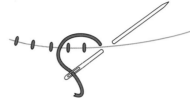

running stitch

backstitch

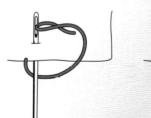

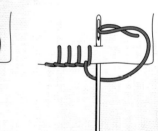

blanket stitch

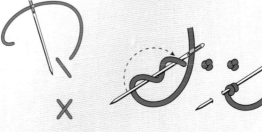

cross stitch   french knot   satin stitch

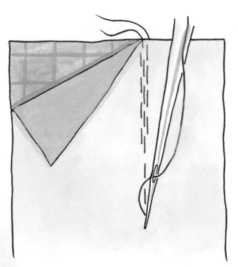

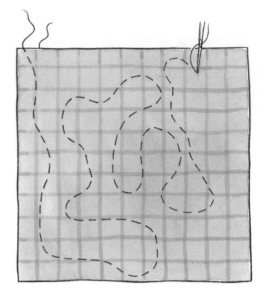

figure 1

figure 2

MACHINE STITCHING

Unless you opt for glue, machine stitching is the easiest, fastest way to permanently join fabric shapes. Follow these basic steps:

1

Backstitch at the start of the seam line by sewing forward for ¼ inch (0.3 cm), in reverse back to the beginning, and then forward again (see figure1).

2

Machine stitch along the seam line using the recommended seam allowance width (the seam allowance is the fabric between the seam line and edge), removing pins as they get close to the needle. The instructions in this book give you the suitable seam allowance width for each project. Always press the seam allowances open unless the instructions give you different advice. Let the machine do the work of pulling the fabric along.

3

To stitch around a corner, keep the needle down at the corner point and pivot the fabric. Backstitch at the end of the seam line so that the stitching doesn't unravel.

Free-Motion Stitching

This is the perfect technique for anyone who likes to draw outside the lines because you're free to stitch through one or more fabric layers in any way that strikes your fancy. Really. You place fabric on the sewing machine bed with some of it under the needle and stitch while shifting the fabric forward, back, sideways, diagonally, and in circles or swirls. The movements can be random (see figure 2) or create a design.

Satin Stitching

When zigzag stitches are really close together (dense) and set to any width other than 0, you have satin stitching. It looks just like the hand-embroidered version, except that the stitching is a uniform length and width along the entire line.

Straight Stitching

Every machine has this stitch because it's used more than any other. Unless the instructions in this book give you a different setting, use a medium-length straight stitch—about 2.5 mm or 12 spi (stitches per inch). Whatever the system on your machine, you'll be in good shape if you dial into something in the middle of the offered range. Set the stitch width to 0.

Topstitching

There's nothing mysterious about this—it's just straight stitching worked with the right side up, usually through several fabric thicknesses, and positioned near an edge or seam line.

Zigzag Stitching

If you don't own pinking shears, you can use medium-length, wide-width zigzag stitching to prevent fraying along fabric edges (see figure 3).

MAKING BUTTONHOLES

Machine stitching around a buttonhole prevents the cut fabric edges from stretching and fraying. Most sewing machines make a buttonhole with little more than a twist of a dial and a presser foot change. Follow the instructions in the manual for your sewing machine to make a buttonhole.

If you have infinite patience you can hand sew a buttonhole by cutting through the fabric and then edging the opening with close-set blanket stitches.

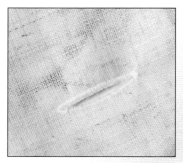

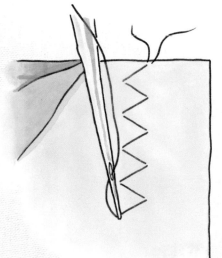

figure 3

Tip!

Decorative snaps are an excellent option if you hate making buttonholes. Kit instructions tell you exactly what to do. What the instructions might not tell you is that it's a good idea to reinforce the back of the fabric with medium or heavyweight fusible interfacing. Also, make the hole in the fabric as small as possible.

pillowcase memory

My favorite pillowcase never officially belonged to me, although I coveted it fiercely. When I was young, my brother had the most spectacular Star Wars sheet set; I'm talking Chewbacca (my favorite), Princess Leia, R2-D2, and the whole gang. I remember the pillowcase having particular appeal; it stayed especially colorful while the rest of the sheet set seemed to fade with use. When my brother decided he was too grown-up for themed sheets—I had made do, for a time, with my Strawberry Shortcake set—I assumed I was next in line. However, the next time I saw that case, it was underneath my other "brother"—a wonderfully persnickety dachshund named Barney—in his doggy bed. Years later, I had my revenge. I took the whole set, case and sheets, off with me to college. I still use the sheets from time to time—almost 30 years since my brother got them—although these days, the pillowcase usually ends up being lovingly washed...er, licked...by my people-bed-loving pooch, Baby.

Amanda Carestio

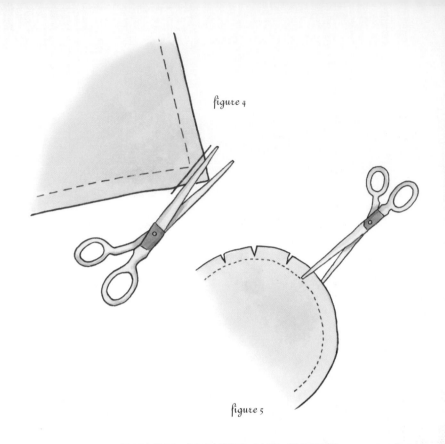

figure 4

figure 5

CLIPPING CORNERS AND CURVES

A well-made seam is flat and smooth when it's right side out. (The exceptions, of course, are intentionally gathered fabric (see page 27) and other special effects, but we're not dealing with that here.) Seam allowances can mess with this perfection because these bits of excess fabric are either bunched up or stretched out on the underside, particularly at corners and curves. The instructions tell you when the seam allowances for a corner or curve shouldn't be clipped. The solutions to these problems are simple.

Corners

Snip diagonally across the tip of a corner to remove excess seam allowance (see figure 4). Stay more than 1/8 inch (0.3 cm) away from the stitching.

Curves

Use the tips of your sharpest scissors to snip through the seam allowances perpendicular to the seam line. Make sure that you snip to—but not through—the stitching (see figure 5). Space the snips 1/2 inch (1.3 cm) apart along the curved portion of the seam line. Make more snips if the seam line still isn't smooth.

MAKING A CASING

There's nothing mysterious about a casing: It's just a bit of fabric that creates a channel to guide and hold elastic or a drawstring. Project instructions may tell you to turn under different amounts of fabric, but the process, explained here, remains the same.

--------(1)--------

Fuse a ¼-inch wide strip (0.6 cm) of paper-backed fusible web along the right side of the upper edge of the fabric. (If desired, you can skip this process and just pin or baste the fabric layers together in step 3.)

--------(2)--------

Press under the top ⅜ inch (0.95 cm) of fabric.

--------(3)--------

Measure down 2 inches (5.1 cm) from the folded edge and press this to the wrong side (see figure 6). Peel the paper off the fusible web and press again.

--------(4)--------

Sew a line of straight stitching close to the lower folded edge, leaving an opening to insert the elastic or drawstring. You may not need this opening: check the project instructions to find out if the opening is created with a buttonhole or a gap in a vertical seam that goes through the casing.

--------(5)--------

Pull the elastic or drawstring through the casing using a bodkin or large safety pin. Sew the opening closed unless it's an opening for a drawstring.

BINDING AN EDGE

You can wrap a strip of fabric around the edges of one or more fabric layers to create a clean, sturdy edge that's also decorative. Start with a binding strip that you make yourself. (Store-bought single-fold tape can also be used in much the same way.)

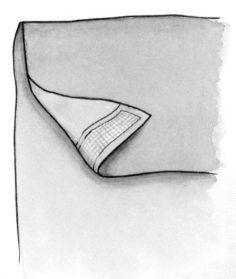

figure 6

Making a Binding Strip

--------(1)--------

Cut a strip of fabric on the bias for the binding. The instructions will indicate the width you need, which is usually twice the finished width plus two seam allowances. The strip needs to be long enough to cover the entire edge, so you may need to cut a couple of strips and sew them together end-to-end.

--------(2)--------

Fold the strip in half along the length, right side out.

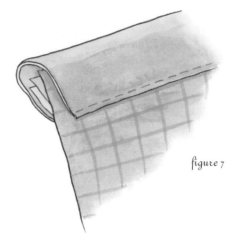

figure 7

Attaching Binding to an Edge

1

Sew the matched edges of the strip to the right side of the project along the fabric edge.

2

Wrap the binding over the seam allowances or fabric edge to the underside of the project so that the folded edge extends barely beyond the seamline you just made (see figure 7).

3

Pin the binding in place. If you find yourself back at the start of the binding (when you're covering an armhole, for example), cut the binding so that the end extends ½ inch (1.3 cm) beyond the starting point. Fold under ⅛ inch (0.3 cm) of the raw end and pin the end over the start of the binding.

4

Sew along the inner folded edge of the binding through all thicknesses and with the right side of the project face up.

GATHERING FABRIC

These steps explain how to gather fabric at an edge, but you can easily adapt the process to gather any part of a fabric piece.

――――――――――――――――（1）――――――――――――――――

Set your machine's straight stitch length to the longest possible. Sew two parallel lines of stitching, the first ¼ inch (6 mm) from the edge and the second ⅞ inch (22 mm) away from the edge. Leave 3-inch (7.6 cm) thread tails at the beginning and end of each stitching line.

――――――――――――――――（2）――――――――――――――――

Wind the thread tails around a pin inserted at the start of the stitching lines. Pull on the thread tails at the end of the stitching lines until the fabric edge is drawn in to the desired length.

――――――――――――――――（3）――――――――――――――――

Set your machine for a regular length straight stitch. Pin the gathered edge to the fabric piece you want to join, with both right sides together. (Backstitch at the beginning and end of this permanent seam!) Sew the pieces together with the recommended seam allowance width. Remove the pin at the start of the gathering. Pull on the gathering thread tails until the gathering stitches are removed.

ADDING TRIMS

Trims can be added while you're putting together a project, or added afterward. Think beyond a simple edging and consider attaching a fabric puff called a yo-yo (see Cupcake Cuffs, page 86) or a crocheted motif.

Although there are many types of trims, when it comes to the way they're attached, they can be broken down into two categories: One type has a plain or unfinished edge that's meant to be trapped in a seam, while all of the others have completely finished edges so they'll look great sewn anywhere on a fabric surface.

pillowcase
MEMORY

My maternal grandma always had an embroidery project going. More often than not, these projects were pillowcases—millions and millions of pillowcases—and I watched her work. I can picture her sewing box, thimbles, and, of course, her stork scissors. My grandma's embroidery spanned her lifetime, from childhood into her eighties. She embroidered on white, 100-percent cotton pillowcases that were stamped with a design, usually a floral. She picked unfinished ones up at garage sales and thrift stores or was given them by friends. My grandma made a pair of pillowcases for each of her children and grandchildren. I received a pair with satin-stitched orange flowers and a multitude of French knots.

Katy Hanson

pillowcase MEMOry

My favorite pillowcase is one that I had as a child. It's a Wamsutta "Lustercale" case with Mary Poppins (circa 1964) sitting sidesaddle on a beautifully decorated merry-go-round horse. Jane and Michael are on their own steeds in front of and behind her. I loved looking at the bright cheerful colors and imagining myself on a horse of my own. I loved the case's softness (from so many washings) and how fresh it smelled after my mother hung it on the line. Somewhere around middle school, the pillowcase got buried in the back of the linen closet while I moved on to more "grown-up" things. When I discovered it a few years ago while helping my parents move to a new house, I was immediately taken back—and the pillowcase was taken home. My two boys (three and five) are currently fascinated with Mary Poppins, and I've been tempted to share the case with them...but maybe not just yet!

Mary Gaston

figure 8

Appliqué

Any trim—even if it has one plain edge—can be attached anywhere on the surface of a fabric if you like the effect. All you do is baste or pin it in the desired position, and then sew it to the background (see figure 8). You can use hand-worked appliqué stitches or machine straight, satin, or zigzag stitching.

Seam Line Insertion

Simply place the trim on top of a fabric piece, both right sides up, with the plain edge of the trim aligned with the edge of the material. Place the second fabric piece on top, right side down, and sew the seam (see figure 9).

MAKING A NARROW HEM

This simple, unobtrusive hem is so easy that you'll end up using it all the time. If flimsy fabric gives you trouble just spray on some starch or stabilizer before you begin. Heavier fabrics are easier to handle if you fuse a narrow strip of paper-backed fusible web along the right side of the raw edge, pull off the protective paper, and then start step 1.

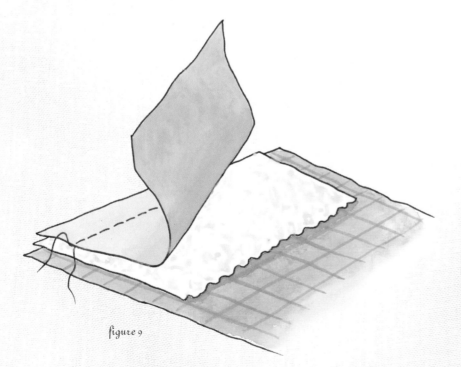

figure 9

1

Press under ¼ inch (0.6 cm) along the raw edge.

2

Make a second fold along the same edge, to encase the previous fold. This second fold usually ends up being slightly more than ¼ inch (0.6) wide.

3

Use a machine straight stitch to sew along the innermost fold, through all of the fabric layers.

...Wear

Layer Cake Apron

Delectable tiers of beautiful embroidered edgework whet your appetite in this ruffled creation.

Designed by Lee-Ann Edwards

what you need

4 vintage
standard pillowcases

Thread to match the
pillowcases and trim

39-inch (99 cm) lengths of trim for
each ruffle you want to embellish

8 vintage buttons, ½ to 1 inch
(1.3 to 2.5 cm) in diameter

SEAM ALLOWANCE
¼ inch (6 mm)
unless noted otherwise

Project Instructions

1

Prepare the Backing

Cut off the closed end of one of the pillowcases 15 inches (38.1 cm) below the seam line. Set aside the hemmed portion (the tube) to make one of the ruffles in step 2.

Cut off the top seam and just a bit of fabric at the sides to obtain two equal-size rectangles. Set one rectangle aside for the waistband.

On the remaining rectangle (the backing), finish the sides and bottom with pinking shears, machine zigzag stitching, or narrow hems (see page 29).

2

Cut the Ruffles

Measure up 8 inches (20.3 cm) from the open (hemmed) edge of all three remaining pillowcases and the tube leftover from the previous step.

Place each of the four tubes face down on a flat surface with the sides to your right and left. Make a vertical cut the entire way through the upper layer of every one (see figure 1).

3

Prepare the Ruffles

Cut all four pieces to 38 inches (96.5 cm) long, centering any existing motifs.

Narrow hem all of the short ends.

4

Cut the Waistband

Cut the waistband to the same width as the backing plus ½ inch (1.3 cm) and 5 inches (12.7 cm) deep.

figure 1

5

Prepare the Ties

Cut two 42 x 4½-inch (106.7 x 11.4 cm) lengths from any of the pillowcases.

Narrow hem the two long edges of both ties. Fold under ¼ inch (6 mm) on a short end of each tie. Bring this end over to meet the start of one of the long hemmed edges and stitch it in place (see figure 2).

Press—then baste—a 1-inch (2.5 cm) deep pleat at the raw short end of each tie (see figure 2 again).

6

Apply the Trim

Sew trim to the lower edges of the ruffles as desired.

7

Plan the Ruffle Placement

Draw a straight line across the width of the backing on the right side and 1 inch (2.5 cm) above the hemline. Draw three more lines above the first, spacing them 4 inches (10.2 cm) apart.

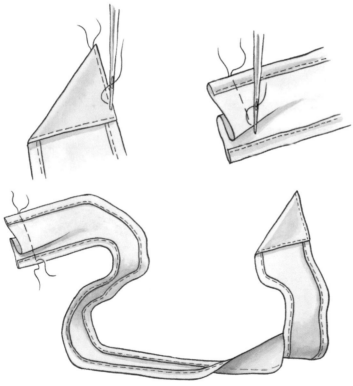

figure 2

The cutting edge

Your pillowcases don't have to be perfect! Look for ones that have edgings you love. You can usually cut around stains or holes on the upper portion. In fact, only the bottom 8 inches (20.3 cm) are used on three of the pillowcases, so you will have plenty of extra fabric to work with.

figure 3

8

Attach the Ruffles

Gather the upper edge of each ruffle (see page 27).

Pin the lowest ruffle on the backing, both right sides up, with the ruffle's upper edge along the backing's lowest drawn line (see figure 3).

Topstitch the ruffle to the backing ¼ inch (6 mm) from the gathered edge. Press it and then zigzag stitch over the raw edges. Sew a ruffle to each of the other lines on the backing.

9

Attach the Waistband

Press under ¼ inch (6 mm) along one long raw edge and both short ends of the Waistband. Sew the remaining raw edge to the upper edge of the top ruffle (it's attached to the backing) with the right sides together and the excess backing extending beyond the ruffle's upper edge (see figure 4).

10

Finish the Waistband

Fold and pin the upper half of the waistband to the wrong side so that the long, folded edge extends just past the seam line you just stitched.

Slide the unhemmed, pleated end of each apron tie inside an end of the waistband. Make sure the right side of both ties are facing out. Sew across the ends of the waistband and sew the long edge to the waist.

11

Attach Buttons

Embellish the apron by sewing buttons to the front as desired.

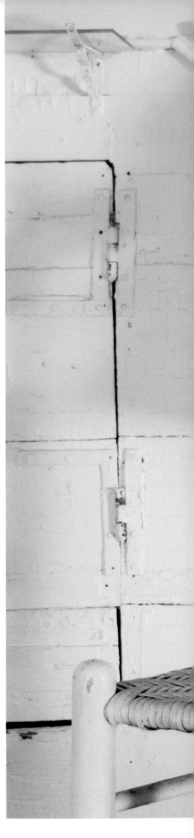

figure 4

pillowcase pinafore

Perfect for showing off vintage or new embroidered pillowcases,
this sweet garment is meant to be worn for a while; first as a dress, then as a top!

Designed by Debbie Brisson

Project Instructions

Prepare the Templates

Cut off the seam at the closed end and just a bit of fabric at each side to obtain two equal-size rectangles from the pillowcase. Fold both pillowcase pieces in half lengthwise. Place the templates (page 127) along the folds as noted on them, with the front and front facing on one rectangle and the back and back facing on the other, making sure that the bottom of the body pieces are aligned with the bottom (hemmed edge) of the rectangles. Cut out the shapes. Don't cut off the hemmed edge of the pillowcase!

Prepare the Facings

Clip along the curves at the bottom of each neck facing (see page 24).

Press up ⅜ inch (0.95 cm) along the bottom edges, working on a small section at a time to make sure you're getting an even fold.

Place the front neck facing and the back neck facing wrong sides together, and sew one of the side seams using a ¼-inch (6 mm) seam allowance.

Fold the piece wrong side out along the seam line and lightly press the seam flat.

Make a second seam at the same place as the first one, this time with the right sides together and using a ⅜-inch (9.5 mm) seam allowance. This encases the raw edges of the previous stitching to complete a French seam. Join the other side seam in the same way.

Join the Pinafore Front and Back

Starting at the bottom and working up to the armhole, sew the front and back pieces together at one side seam. Join the other side seam, also from bottom to top, so the hemline remains even. Don't trim off any of the excess crocheted edging or other fancy trim at the corners. Wait until the pinafore is finished so you can make sure everything looks right and you don't need to rework anything.

What You Need

Embroidered standard pillowcase, no less than 29 x 20 inches (73.7 x 50.8 cm)

Thread to match the pillowcase

4 snaps, each ⁷⁄₁₆ inch (1.1 cm)

Finished Size

Fits a child 18 to 24 months old

SEAM ALLOWANCE
⅜ inch (9.5 mm)
unless noted otherwise

Oui! Oui!

You don't have to use a French seam for the sides. If you'd rather take the easier route, just sew up the sides using a ⅜-inch (9.5 mm) seam allowance. Pink or zigzag stitch along the raw edges so they don't fray.

Button Up

You can use a button in place of each snap; simply sew two buttonholes in each top strap. Other options are metal eyehooks or hook and loop tape...whatever works for your little one. Debbie Brisson uses snaps for pinafores she makes for a treasured member of the family. Her niece loves to tear open hook and loop tape and went through a phase where she was biting the buttons off everything. Kids.

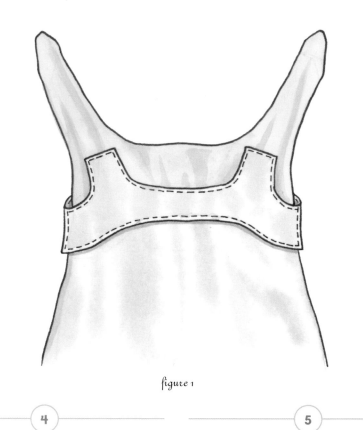

figure 1

4

Attach the Facing

Turn the joined front and back (the body) right side out. Place the joined facings—inside out—over the body. The neckline edges fit together smoothly, and the right sides are together.

Pin together the neckline, strap, and armhole edges (see figure 1). Sew them as pinned using a ⅜-inch (9.5 mm) seam allowance. Clip through the curves and flip the facing inside the dress.

5

Finishing the Facing

Press the neck and straps flat. After checking the appearance and fit, trim any excess edging out of the corners and then topstitch ¼ inch (6 mm) in from all of the seams you just made.

The side seams of the facing and the body should line up. If you want, you can stitch a short upper section of those two seams together to help keep the facing flat.

6

Add the Closures

Attach the snap parts as marked on the pattern. This arrangement allows you to adjust the fit so the pinafore can be worn as a dress first and a top later, as your vintage-loving fashionista grows.

sunkissed tunic

Summertime, and the livin'
is easy in a crisp tunic top.
String straps tie it together
and an elastic waist ensures
the perfect fit.

Designed by Carissa Adams

What you need

Standard pillowcase

Thread to match
the pillowcase and bias tape

70 inches (76.2 cm)
of extra-wide double-fold bias tape

Length of non-roll elastic
to equal your underbust measurement
plus 2 inches (5.1 cm),
1/4 inch (6 mm) wide

Safety pin

58 inches (147.3 cm)
of decorative string or ribbon,
width as desired

SEAM ALLOWANCE
1/2 inch (13 mm) unless noted otherwise

Take the challenge
with this exclusive
online bonus project at
www.larkbooks.com/crafts

Project Instructions

1

Cut the Armholes

Cut off the seam at the closed end of the pillowcase to create a tube. Bring the two long sides together to make a lengthwise fold.

With the cut edge away from you and the fold to your right, cut out a curved piece 2 1/2 inches deep (6.4 cm) and 7 1/4 inches long (18.4 cm). You don't have to take exact measurements: Just eyeball the shape and go for it! Cut along the lines through all the layers and then unfold the piece. Figure 1 shows the pillowcase with the armholes cut.

2

Cut off the Top

Measure down 4 1/4 inches (10.8 cm) from the bottom of the armhole, and cut all the way across the pillowcase to make the bodice. The hemmed portion of the pillowcase is the bottom. Bind the armholes with the extra-wide double-fold bias tape (see page 26).

3

Make the Waist Casing

Turn the bodice inside out. With right sides together, sew the bodice to the bottom at the previously cut edges. Turn the garment right side out.

Press the seam allowances toward the bottom. Sew the seam allowance raw edges flat against the bottom (see figure 2). (To create a straight seam as you sew, let the left edge of the presser foot glide along the fabric edges.) End the seam 1 inch (2.5 cm) before reaching the starting point. This gap is an opening for inserting the elastic. Turn the garment right side out.

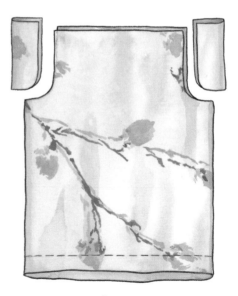

figure 1

4

Insert the Elastic

Measure around your chest just below your bust. Add 2 inches (2.5 cm), and cut the elastic to this length. Attach a safety pin to one end and push it through the casing. Slide your fingers along the casing to make sure the elastic isn't twisted. After you've removed the safety pin, overlap the ends, pin them together, and stitch back and forth a few times to secure them. Sew the casing opening closed.

5

Finish the Neckline

Make a casing (see page 25) at the top raw edge of both the front and back parts of the bodice. The first fold is ¼ inch (6 mm), and the second fold is ½ inch (1.3 cm).

Cut the decorative string or ribbon in half and feed a length through each of the casings for shoulder ties.

figure 2

Tunic: Take 2!

Feeling inspired? Add a pocket or some ruffles, and turn your adult tunic into a girl's dress. The measurements and instructions are the same, and drawstring shoulder straps make the garment's length adjustable—it's really that simple.

sweet pleats

Neat little gathers and button embellishments add extra charm to this darling sundress.

Designed by Vanessa Greenhow

What you need

Standard pillowcase

Thread to match the pillowcase,
bias tape, and rickrack;
and to contrast the pillowcase

1 yard (0.9 m) of double-fold bias tape,
½ inch (1.3 cm) wide

Length of rickrack to match
child's upper chest measurement,
½ inch (1.3 cm) wide

3 yards (2.7 m) of double-fold bias tape,
¼ inch (6 mm) wide

3 buttons, ½ to 1 inch
(1.3 to 2.5 cm) wide

SEAM ALLOWANCE
½ inch (1.3 cm)
unless noted otherwise

Project Instructions

1

Cut the Pillowcase

Measure from your child's shoulder down the body to the place where you want the dress to end. Measure this distance on the pillowcase, starting at the open edge, and then cut straight across the width of the pillowcase through both layers.

The cut edge of this body piece is the top of the dress. The seam along the side of the pillowcase will be the body's center back. If your body piece has two vertical seams, make these the side seams on your dress.

2

Sew the Center Pleat

Turn the body wrong side out and press a crease along the center front. Draw a 6-inch-long (15.2 cm) line parallel to—and 1 inch (2.5 cm) away from—the crease. Sew along the line through both layers using the matching thread (see figure 1).

figure 1

3

Topstitch the Pleat

Open the pleat. Press it flat and centered on the stitching line. Turn the body right side out. Switch to the contrasting thread and topstitch ¼ inch (6 mm) away from the pleat seam on both sides (see figure 2).

4

Make Side Pleats

Turn the body wrong side out. To make box pleats on both sides of the one just completed, start by drawing a line parallel to—and 2 inches (5.1 cm) out from—the center of the finished pleat. Continue making pleats until the upper body circumference is 3 inches (7.6 cm) wider than your child's upper chest. Stop when you have the same number of pleats on both sides of the center front.

5

Make the Armholes

Refold the body by matching the center front and center back. Draw and cut armholes through all four layers and then open the fold, as shown in figure 1 on page 42. Make the armholes 1¾ inches (4.4 cm) deep and 4¼ inches (10.8 cm) long.

6

Finish and Embellish

Bind the body's upper edges with the wide double-fold bias tape using matching thread. Sew the rickrack below the tape.

Bind the raw armhole edges with the narrow bias tape and matching thread (see page 26), leaving at least 10 inches (25.4 cm) extending beyond the top edges for ties.

Sew the buttons near the hem on the front.

figure 2

Tailor Made

Go ahead and change the pleat measurements to put your personal stamp on this dress and tweak the fit. You can vary the pleat width, the distance between each pleat, and the number of pleats to best showcase the fabric and achieve the desired chest measurement for your little girl.

Morning Glory

Want to feel like a queen
in the morning? Slip into
a kimono made from two
king-size pillowcases.

Designed by Joan K. Morris

Project Instructions

1

Make the Body

Place one of the pillowcases flat in front of you with the open end at the bottom. Cut vertically along the center of the top layer only, from the hem through the closed end.

Cut along the closed end for 3 inches (7.6 cm) in each direction from the vertical center cut.

Measure down 12 inches (30.5 cm) from the closed end, along the vertical cut. Lightly draw a line on both sides from this point to the end of the 3-inch (7.6 cm) cuts at the top (see figure 1). Cut along the lines to create the V-neck.

2

Cut the Sleeves

Cut 16 inches (40.6 cm) off the second pillowcase, measuring up from the open end. Save the top, closed end for the belt.

Cut along the sides so you have two 20 x 16-inch pieces (50.8 x 40.6 cm), with the hem along the bottom of both rectangular sleeves.

3

Sew the Underarms

Fold one of the sleeve pieces lengthwise with the right sides together and the hem at the bottom. Sew from the hem to the top edge using a ¼-inch (6 mm) seam allowance. This is the underarm seam. Press the seam allowances to one side. Make the second sleeve.

4

Add the Bias Tape

Turn the sleeves right sides out. Use a 22-inch (55.9 cm) length of the bias tape to bind the hem edge of each sleeve (see page 26).

Stitch bias tape onto the edge of the body.

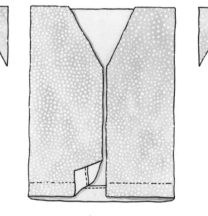

figure 1

What You Need

2 king-size pillowcases, no less than 40½ x 20 inches (102.8 x 50.8 cm)

Thread to match the pillowcase, bias tape, and trim

8 yards (7.3 m) of double-fold bias tape, ¼ inch (6 mm) wide

7 yards (6.4 m) of floral trim, any width

SEAM ALLOWANCE
½ inch (1.3 cm)
unless noted otherwise

figure 2

6

Insert the Sleeves

Open (or cut) 9¾ inches (24.8 cm) of both sides of the body starting at each shoulder (the closed end) and working toward the hem. These are the armholes. Turn the body wrong side out. Insert one of the sleeves inside a body armhole with the right sides together (see figure 3). Pin and then sew the raw edges together around the armhole. Make sure the underarm seam lines are aligned with the bottom of the body's armhole.

Press the seam allowances toward the body. Turn the body and sleeves right side out and topstitch around the armholes, on the body side, to secure the seam allowances.

8

Sew the Belt

Fold in the piece along the center fold line to make the belt ¾ inch (1.9 cm) wide.

Join the open lengthwise folds by sewing close to the matched folds. Sew a length of the trim on top of one side of the belt, folding the trim ends around each end of the belt and sewing them down.

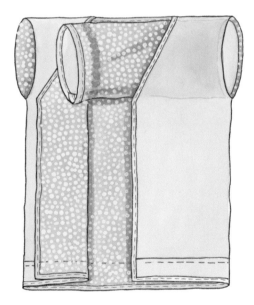

figure 3

5

Attach the Trim

Place the trim 1 inch (2.5 cm) above a sleeve's hem at the underarm seam. Sew across the end with zigzag stitching to hold it in place.

Sew the trim in place all the way around the sleeve, stopping short 2 inches (5.1 cm) from the end. Cut off the excess trim so that it overlaps the start of the trim. Fold under the end and sew it down with zigzag stitching (see figure 2). Attach trim to the other sleeve.

Sew trim to the bottom and neckline of the body.

7

Prepare the Belt Fabric

Cut across the remaining pillowcase tube to create a flat piece of fabric.

Cut along the width of the remaining pillowcase to make enough 3-inch-wide (7.6 cm) pieces for a length that's 60 inches (152.4 cm) long. If needed, sew the short ends together to make the long piece and press the seam allowances open.

Fold and press the belt in half lengthwise with the right side out. Open the fold and press in the raw edges so they match at the center fold. Take care not to flatten the first press line.

Li'L BiRdie

Your little chickadee never looked so chic! Ribbon, rickrack,

and a birdie appliqué make this dress sing.

Designed by Stacy Dinkel

What you need

Standard pillowcase

Thread to contrast pillowcase

42 inches (106.7 cm) of ribbon in
two different colors and width as desired

42 inches (106.7 cm) of rickrack,
½ inch (1.3 cm) wide

5-inch (12.7 cm) square
of coordinating fabric

12 inches (30.5 cm) of elastic,
¾ inch (1.9 cm) wide

Safety pin

60 inches (152.4 cm) of bias tape

SEAM ALLOWANCE
⅝ inch (15 mm)
unless noted otherwise

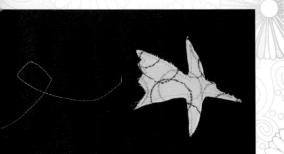

Project Instructions

1

Cut the Pillowcase

To determine the dress's overall length, measure your child from the shoulder to the place where you want the dress to end. Mark this length on the pillowcase, measuring up from the open end. At the desired distance, cut straight across the width of the pillowcase, through both layers. This cut edge is the top of the body.

2

Shape the Armholes

Bring the two long sides of the body together to make a lengthwise fold.

With the cut edge away from you and the fold to your right, draw and then cut the curved piece. Make the shape 2 inches (5.2 cm) deep and 3 inches (7.6 cm) long for a small child. For a larger child, it can be 3 inches (7.6 cm) deep and 4 inches (10.2 cm) long. Unfold the pillowcase (see figure 1).

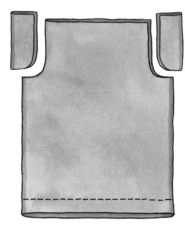

figure 1

3

Add Embellishments

Sew both ribbons, side by side, around the body near the bottom, using the photo as a guide. Sew the rickrack on top.

4

Appliqué the Birdie

Make a template for the birdie (see page 126). Cut the shape from the contrasting fabric square. Pin the shape right side up on the front of the body. Machine straight stitch around the perimeter of the shape, and use the same stitch to create the bird's flight pattern.

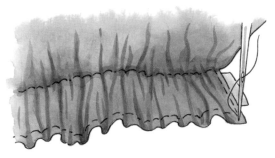

figure 2

5

Gather the Neckline

Switch to the matching thread. Sew a casing (see page 25) at both of the top edges. The first fold is ¼ inch (0.6 cm), and the second fold is 1 inch (2.5 cm).

Cut the elastic into two 6-inch (15.2 cm) pieces. Attach the safety pin to one end of an elastic piece, and pull it through one of the casings, making sure the elastic's trailing end isn't also pulled into the casing. Stitch across the ends of the casing to hold the elastic ends in place (see figure 2). If necessary, trim off any excess elastic at the ends. Insert and secure the other length of elastic in the remaining casing.

6

Bind the Armholes

Cut the bias tape into two pieces. Switch to matching thread and sew the bias tape around a raw armhole edge (see page 26), leaving at least 10 inches (25.4 cm) extending beyond the top edges to form the ties (see figure 3). Finish the other armhole in the same way.

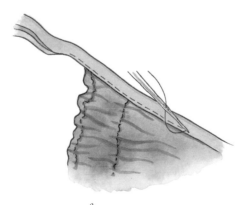

figure 3

simply Red

Pin tucks and ruffles bring sophistication to this easy afternoon project.

Designed by Regina Lord

Standard pillowcase with a hem at least 3 inches (7.6 cm) deep

Thread to match or coordinate with the pillowcase

Pinking shears

Twill tape or ribbon, twice as long as your waist measurement and ½ inch (1.3 cm) wide

Safety pin

finished size

You can make a skirt that will comfortably fit 34- to 38-inch (86.4 to 96.5 cm) hips, depending on your pillowcase size. Don't fret if your pillowcase is too large or small: check out the solutions at the end of step 3.

SEAM ALLOWANCE
½ inch (1.3 cm)
unless noted otherwise

Project Instructions

1

Cut the Skirt Body

Cut off the seam at the closed end of the pillowcase. This cut edge is the waist.

Measure from your waist (or just below the waist if you prefer) to the place where you want the skirt to end. Add 2½ inches (6.4 cm). Measure this same distance on the pillowcase, starting at the cut edge, and then cut straight across the width of the pillowcase through both layers.

2

Cut the Ruffle

Cut the seam off the side of the leftover fabric tube. (If the opposite side also has a seam, cut if off as well.) Also cut off the edge of the hemline (see figure 1).

Cut the two (or four) strips so they're 3 inches (7.6 cm) wide.

3

Check the Fit

Try on the body to check the fit. The total width around the pillowcase should be about 4 inches (10.2 cm) larger than your hip measurement.

If the body is snug, add a coordinating or matching panel (from a second pillowcase) down each side. If it feels too loose, turn the tube wrong side out and sew new side seams using deeper seam allowances.

The side of the tube that has a seam is the center back. If your tube has two vertical seams, make these the side seams on your skirt.

4

Add a Buttonhole Opening

Fold the body (the largest tube) in half vertically so the center front is at the folded edge. (If you have side seams, bring these together. If the tube has only one seam, this is the center back so place it at a fold; the opposite fold is the center front.) Mark the center front fold 2¼ inches (5.7 cm) from the top edge. Open the tube and make a horizontal ½-inch (1.3 cm) buttonhole that's centered on this mark.

5

Make the Waist Casing

Make a casing (see page 25) with a fold that's ½ inch (1.3 cm), followed by another fold that's 1 inch (2.5 cm). When you sew the casing, make sure the buttonhole remains in the center.

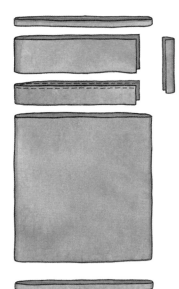

figure 1

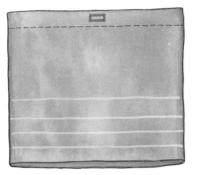

figure 2

6

Make the First Pintuck

With the body right side out, draw horizontal lines 2, 3, 4, and 5 inches (5.1, 7.6, 10.2, and 12.7 cm) from the bottom edge, all around the outside (see figure 2).

Fold under the bottom of the skirt along the uppermost line. Press along the fold. Topstitch around the entire body ⅛ inch (3 mm) from the fold line.

Unfold the lower portion of the body, which was pressed under.

7

Add More Pintucks

Make another pintuck along the next two drawn lines, each time topstitching ½ inch (1.3 cm) from the fold line. Make the last pintuck by topstitching ⅛ inch (3 mm) from the fold line.

Press all of the pintucks toward the bottom of the body.

8

Prepare the Ruffle

Sew together the short ends of the ruffle pieces with the right sides facing. Press the seam allowances open. Trim the upper long edge and seam allowances with pinking shears.

Make a narrow hem at the lower edge.

9

Gather the Ruffle

Sew two lines of gathering stitches along the upper edge (see page 27). Before gathering the fabric by drawing up these stitches, divide the top and bottom edges into quarters that are marked with pins.

With the right sides together, pin the ruffle's gathered edge to the bottom of the body, matching the sides, center front, and center back with the pins. Adjust the ruffle gathers to fit the body edge. Sew the pieces together, press the seam allowances toward the body, and topstitch just above the seam line using a zigzag stitch.

10

Insert the Drawstring

Sew across the ends of the ribbon or twill tape so the ends don't ravel. Attach the safety pin to one end of the ribbon or twill tape. Thread it into the buttonhole, through the waist casing, and out the buttonhole.

You're in charge

How full do want the ruffle to be? Before you join the short ends, cut the ruffle strip to a length that will give you exactly what you want: a 60-inch (152.4 cm) strip will yield a soft ruffle. A 70-inch (177.8 cm) strip was used for the skirt shown in the photos. For a generous ruffle, cut the strip to 80 inches (203.2 cm).

Ditto Darling!

Mothers, daughters, and sisters will love these coordinating pants!

Designed by Joan K. Morris

What You Need

2 standard, solid-colored pillowcases for mom*

Standard, printed pillowcase: 1 for mom and 2 for daughter

Pull-on pants patterns for mom and daughter (see the Go Your Own Way sidebar on page 63)

Thread to match the pillowcases and ribbon

2⅔ yards (2.4 m) of ribbon, ⅞ inch (2.2 cm) wide

1⅓ yards (1.2 m) of small-ball fringe for daughter

1⅔ yards (1.5 m) of elastic, 1 inch (2.5 cm) wide

*Save your leftover solid-colored pillowcase fabric for the daughter's pants.

Finished Size

The size you make is only limited by the width across the narrowest pillowcase that you plan to use for the pants. (The width of the pillowcases for the contrasting bands won't affect the fit.) Measure across a pillowcase when it's laid flat. Now measure across the widest part of the front and back pattern pieces. The pillowcase must be the same width or wider.

SEAM ALLOWANCE
As directed in the pants patterns unless noted otherwise in these instructions

Mom's Lounge Pants Instructions

1
Make the Yardage

Open both of the solid-colored pillowcases and one of the printed pillowcases by cutting off the seams at the closed ends and one side seam on each of them. These will be used for the fronts and backs.

Cut across the width of the open, printed pillowcase to obtain two 40 x 10-inch (101.6 x 25.4 cm) lengths. These are the bands.

2
Prepare the Bands

Fold under ½ inch (1.3 cm) along both lengthwise edges of a band. Fold it in half lengthwise. Baste together the loose folded edges (see figure 1). Make the second band the same way.

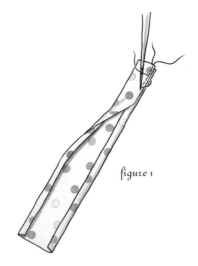

figure 1

3
Attach the Bands

Place the basted edge of a band 1½ inch (3.8 cm) above the hemline on the right side of a solid-colored pillowcase you cut open in the first step. Pin—then machine sew—them together (see figure 2).

Sew the remaining printed band to the other opened, solid-colored pillowcase.

4
Cut the Fronts and Backs

Cut your front and back pattern pieces from the band-trimmed solid-colored yardage by positioning the hemline of the pattern pieces along the bottom of an attached printed Band (see figure 3). Save the leftover solid-colored fabric for the daughter's pants.

5
Trim the Legs

Appliqué (see page 28) the ribbon 1¾ inches (4.4 cm) above the solid-colored hemline on the fronts and backs.

6
Assemble the Fronts and Backs

Sew together the pants as explained in the pattern.

Daughter's Lounge Pants Instructions

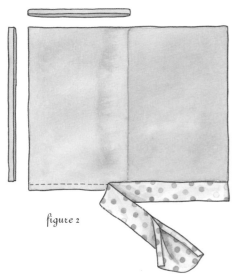

figure 2

figure 3

Make the Yardage

Open both of the remaining printed pillow-cases by cutting off the seams at the closed ends and one side on each of them.

Create the Bands

Piece together enough of the solid-colored leftovers to make two 40 x 10-inch (101.6 x 25.4 cm) lengths.

Fold, press, and baste these lengths to make two contrasting bands in the same way that you made the bands for Mom's pants.

Sew the solid-colored bands to the bottom of the printed pillowcases you cut open.

Attach the Trim

Place a length of the ball fringe under the hem of each band and sew them together. Appliqué the ribbon above the ball fringe.

Finish the Pants

Assemble the fabric pieces the same way that you made Mom's lounge pants.

Go Your Own Way

It's easy to find a suitable pull-on pants pattern for these lounge pants. Just look for a capri or pajama pants pattern that features an elasticized waist, inner and outer leg seams, and straight legs. Avoid any pattern that includes pockets or a fly front.

...show

sherbet purse

Inside-out and outside-in, a reversible candy-colored purse with bamboo handles brings out your best side.

Designed by Cassi Griffin

Project Instructions

1

Cut the Pillowcases

Turn the pillowcases right side out. Cut across the width of both pillowcases 18 inches (45.7 cm) from the closed end. The open end of the pillowcases will not be used. Cut off the side seams and the side folds of both pieces. If necessary, trim the cut edges so that you have two 17-inch-wide (43.2 cm) rectangles with the original, closed-end seams intact. One piece is the lining, and the other is the outer body. Both measure 17 x 36 inches (43.2 x 91.4 cm).

2

Make the Side Seams

Keep the outer body and lining wrong sides out and folded along the existing seam. Handling each piece separately, sew the open sides together for 10 inches (25.4 cm) from the closed end.

3

Make the Lining

Turn the Lining right side out and place it inside the outer body with the right sides together. Push out the bottom corners and match the seam lines and raw edges. At the sides of both shapes, the top 8 inches (20.3 cm) of the lining and the outer body are loose. The bags will be joined at these edges. Sew an 8-inch-long (20.3 cm) portion of the lining to the nearest same-length portion of the outer body. Repeat this for the other three segments.

Pink all of the sewn edges.

4

Attach the Handles

Turn the pieces right side out by pulling them through one of the open top edges. Push the lining into the outer body. Push out the corners and match the edges. On the unsewn top openings, press the outer body and lining under toward each other ⅝ inch (1.6 cm) and edge stitch them together.

Fold 1½ inches (3.8 cm) of the upper edge over one purse handle. Hand or machine-sew over the previous edge stitching to enclose the handle within the fold. Attach the other handle the same way.

What You Need

2 standard pillowcases

Thread to match the pillowcases

Pinking shears

Set of oval (D-shaped) purse handles, 7 x 5 inches (17.8 x 12.7 cm)

SEAM ALLOWANCE
⅝ inch (15 mm)
unless noted otherwise

slip-on Luxe

Case of the blues? Not with these ultra-comfy quilted slippers made with recycled jeans for the soles.

Designed by Valerie Shrader

Project Instructions

---
① Make a Template

Trace the bottom of one of the flip-flops onto the paper. Remove the flip-flop and draw a new line ½ inch (1.3 cm) outside the first, all the way around. Cut out this template along the outer line.

Preshrink the cotton batting as directed by the manufacturer so that your finished slippers won't lose a size (or more!) when washed.

Use the template to cut a left and right sole from the batting, buckram, denim, and fusible batting. Be sure to flip over the template before cutting the second foot shape. Cut a left and right sole lining from the pillowcase (don't use the pillowcase hem).

---
② Layer the Soles

Fuse the fusible batting to the bottom of each cotton batting sole. Working on the left foot and then the right, make a sandwich with the pieces in the following order: denim on the bottom with the wrong side up, buckram, batting with the cotton side up, and the sole lining right side up.

---
③ Quilt the Sole

Install the walking foot (if you have one) on your sewing machine. Make a couple of lines of stitching in the center of each stack to stabilize the piece. Free-motion quilt (see page 22) the rest of the shape as desired.

Sew several times around the entire perimeter of each of sole ½ inch (1.3 cm) from the outer edge.

What You Need

Standard pillowcase

Pair of favorite flip-flops (for measurement)

8½ x 11-inch (21.6 x 27.9 cm) piece of paper

¼ yard (0.3 m) of cotton batting

¼ yard (0.3 m) of buckram

Old denim blue jeans or ¼ yard (0.3 m) of heavyweight denim

¼ yard (0.3 m) of heavyweight fusible batting

Thread to match the pillowcase and trim

Walking foot for your sewing machine (optional)

1 yard (0.9 m) of trim, 2 inches (5.1 cm) wide

SEAM ALLOWANCE
½ inch (13 mm)
unless noted otherwise

Walk This Way

There's a specialty presser foot that makes it easier to sew together multiple (or thick) layers with your sewing machine. Called a "walking foot," it makes sure that the top and bottom layers of fabric (or batting) move through the sewing area at the same speed. There's no slippage, so the pieces are joined together exactly as pinned with hardly any extra effort from you!

slip-on Luxe

4
Construct the Top

Cut two bands from the hemmed portion of the pillowcase, each at least 8 inches (20.3 cm) long. Set the width by trimming along the line of hem stitching. Cut two matching pieces of batting and two pieces of trim to the same length.

Working on one band at a time, make a sandwich with cotton batting on the bottom, the pillowcase band right side up, and the trim centered right side up on top. Sew the trim to the layers using the walking foot (if you have one).

5
Adjust the Fit

Step on one of the soles and place the band across the top of your foot. Trim one side of the slipper top to fit the contour of the bottom, and stitch it in place ½ inch (13 mm) from the edge. Repeat the line of stitching a couple of times.

Step onto the sole once again and adjust the top for the desired fit. Trim the remaining side to fit the sole, and stitch it in place as you did the first side.

Trim close to the lines of stitching around the exterior. Secure the batting to the band with blanket stitches (see page 21). Repeat the fit and seaming to attach the second band.

peekaboo scarf

Reverse appliqué flowers add a special touch to a soft jersey knit scarf with fanciful fringe.

Designed by Beth Sweet

What You Need

3 standard jersey pillowcases:
2 the same color,
1 a contrasting color

Waxed, non-porous paper

Design to stencil, no larger
than 9 x 24 inches (22.9 x 61 cm)

Stencil film, cardboard,
or tracing paper

Craft knife

Liquid fabric paint

Embroidery floss to
match your design*

Embroidery needle

Appliqué scissors (optional)

*Outlining the tulips and stems
took two skeins of medium green,
and one skein each of dark
purple, plum, and rose.

SEAM ALLOWANCE
½ inch (6 mm)
unless noted otherwise

Project Instructions

Prepare the Layers

Cut along the sides of the contrasting pillow-case (what will be the inner pillowcase) and one of the other pillowcases (the outer pillow-case) and open them. Fold and press both pil-lowcases—separately—in half lengthwise.

Ironing jersey pillowcases is a relative concept. This T-shirt-like fabric does not lend itself to crisp, clean edges, so perfection is not mandatory. To keep the inner pillowcase from bunching, stitch along the long edges.

②

Paint Your Design

Pin a layer of waxed paper inside the outer pillowcase.

Cut your design into the stencil film using the craft knife. Transfer the design onto the outer pillowcase with the liquid fabric paint. Let it dry thoroughly before moving on.

③

Join the Layers

Open the painted outer pillowcase, remove the waxed paper, and place the outer pillow-case painted side down. Pin the double-layer inner pillowcase to the top (wrong) side of the painted half of the outer pillowcase. Sew the inner pillowcase to the outer pillowcase along the outermost edge (see figure 1). Do not sew the outer case closed just yet!

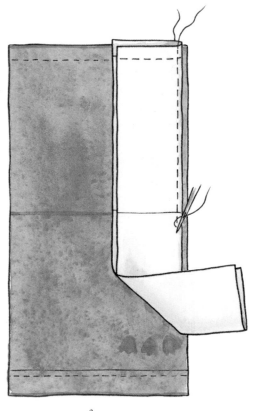

figure 1

4

Complete the Reverse Appliqué

Outline the painted shapes with straight stitches using the embroidery floss and needle. Do this by stitching through the inner pillowcase layers and the front of the outer pillowcase.

Cut away the inside of the painted shapes through the single outer layer of fabric with the craft knife or the appliqué scissors, leaving a thin edge of painted fabric intact (see figure 2). The paint prevents the fabric from unraveling and outlines the shapes.

5

Make Side Seams

Fold the outer pillowcase to sandwich the doubled inner pillowcase with the reverse appliqué exposed. Sew the long edges together with the right sides facing out and the edges raw.

6

Create the Fringe

Embroider the front of the hem area at the open end of the third pillowcase using cross and straight stitches.

Cut across the width of the pillowcase 7 inches (17.9 cm) from the open end. Cut along both sides of the embroidered tube.

Wrap the embroidered end of one of the pieces around one end of the scarf. Sew around the top, bottom, and sides of the hem area, stitching through all of the layers. Fringe the portion of the attached (third) pillowcase extending beyond the embroidery. Repeat these steps to complete the other end of the scarf.

figure 2

Quick on the Draw

You don't have to use a stencil—you can paint your design freehand, if you wish. The scarf shown in the photos features stenciled blooms with freehand stems and leaves. Just remember to keep your designs from becoming too detailed—give yourself enough room to reveal a 1/8-inch (3 mm) painted edge around each shape once you've cut away the shape's center.

Lavender Tote

On your way to a picnic? The beach? The library? This roomy tote carries your goods in style.

Designed by Judi Music

What You Need

Standard vintage cotton
feed-sack pillowcase

1 yard (0.9 m) of
coordinating cotton fabric

1 yard (0.9 m) of medium-weight
fusible interfacing

Thread to match and coordinate
with the pillowcase

Button to complement the flower,
1 inch (2.5 cm) wide

SEAM ALLOWANCE
⅝ inch (15 mm)
unless noted otherwise

Project Instructions

1
Cut the Pieces

Cut the seams off the top and the side of the pillowcase.

Enlarge the patterns on page 128 and make templates. As noted on the patterns, cut the pieces from the pillowcase, cotton fabric, and interfacing.

In addition to the patterns, cut the following pieces from the pillowcase: two 6 x 7-inch (15.2 x 17.8 cm) pockets and four 3 x 22-inch (7.6 x 55.9 cm) handles.

Cut four 3 x 22-inch (7.6 x 55.9 cm) handles from the interfacing.

2
Set the Pleats

Fold two groups of three pleats along the top of both exteriors. Adjust the pleat widths until the top edge is 14 inches (35.6 cm). Stitch over the top of all of the pleats using a ¼-inch (6 mm) seam allowance.

3
Attach the Bands

Sew a straight edge of each band to the pleated edge of each exterior with the right sides together.

Press the seam allowances toward the band and topstitch them close to the seam line.

4
Make the Bag

Sew together the two joined pieces (band and exterior) along the sides and bottom with the right sides together.

At one of the lower corners, bring the side and bottom seam lines together. Sew a straight 4-inch-long (10.2 cm) line across this fold and then cut off the excess at the point (see figure 1). Make the other corner in the same way. Turn the bag right side out.

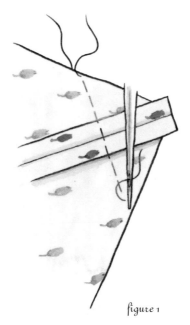

figure 1

⑤
Make the Handles

Fuse interfacing to the wrong side of each handle. Match them as pairs and sew the long edges together with the wrong sides out.

Turn the two handles right side out and iron them flat, being sure to line up the seams. Topstitch the long sides.

Place one of the handles on the outside of the bag with the ends aligned with the raw edges. Sew the ends to the bag's edge using a ¼-inch (6 mm) seam allowance.

⑥
Prepare the Lining

Fuse interfacing to the wrong side of both of the lining pieces.

Match the pocket pieces right sides together and sew around all of the edges, leaving a 2-inch (5.1 cm) opening. Turn the shape right side out. Sew three edges of the pocket to one of the lining pieces.

Sew the lining pieces together with the right sides facing, leaving a 5-inch (12.7 cm) opening at the bottom. Finish the corners as before.

⑦
Attach the Lining

Slip the lining over the purse with the right sides together and the top edges matching. Sew around the entire top edge, making sure that the ends of the handles are flat and caught in the stitching. The lengths of the handles are trapped inside the layers for the time being.

Turn the purse right side out through the opening in the lining. Sew the opening closed. Push the lining into the bag and topstitch the upper edge.

⑧
Make the Flower

Enlarge the petal pattern (see page 128) and make a template. Cut the petal pieces from the pillowcase scraps.

Sew together pairs with the wrong sides out, leaving an opening as marked. Turn them right side out. Fold—and then stitch—a pleat at the open end of all five. Arrange the petals and sew them together. Sew the button in the center to hide the stitches. Sew the flower to the purse.

Placement Makes Perfect

Take a few minutes to think about the placement of your pieces on the pillowcase before cutting them out. Some pieces can be cut entirely from the body of the pillowcase, which is probably a print, or from an area that's a solid color or a complementary print. Every purse you make can be different—even if each one is cut from the same set of pillowcases. Be fussy at this stage so you best utilize the decorative designs that you can find along the edges of old pillowcases.

Sunny Lunchbox

Make every meal a picnic! This clever design includes a roll-up placemat with a pocket for silverware.

Designed by Elizabeth Hartman

Project Instructions

1

Cut the Vinyl

Cut the clear vinyl into one 20 x 15-inch (50.8 x 38.1 cm) piece and two 3 x 12-inch (7.6 x 30.5 cm) pieces.

2

Cut the Materials

Cut off the top seam and side seam of the pillowcase. Cut off the hem at the open end.

From the hem, cut two pieces that will measure 15 x 7 inches (38.1 x 17.8 cm) when opened. Cut both pieces with the hemline (the folded edge, which was the pillowcase's open edge) running along the length of—and centered on—the pieces. These are the drawstring panels.

Cut the following pieces from the remaining pillowcase: one 20 x 15-inch (50.8 x 38.1 cm) exterior panel, one 20 x 15-inch (50.8 x 38.1 cm) lining, and two 3 x 12-inch (7.6 x 30.5 cm) handles.

3

Make the Handles

Fuse the matching vinyl pieces to the right sides of the two handles. Fold each of the long raw edges under ¼ inch (6 mm), using the paper backing to prevent the vinyl from melting onto your iron. Fold both of the handles in half lengthwise with the wrong sides together.

Topstitch the long edges with the white thread and the heavyweight/denim needle. Change your thread to match the rickrack and sew a strip down the center of each handle.

4

Prepare the Exterior Panel

Fuse the last piece of vinyl to the right side of the exterior. Place the paper backing from the vinyl aside to protect your iron later while pressing the vinyl-coated fabric.

5

Make the Drawstring Panels

Sew rickrack over the worn fold line running down the center of both drawstring panels. If your pieces don't have visible fold lines, press a lengthwise crease to create a guide.

Press the entire length of the twill tape in half lengthwise and cut it into four 8-inch (20.3 cm) lengths.

Switch back to the white thread. Slip one short end of a drawstring panel into a piece of the folded tape and sew it in place. Cover the other side of this panel piece and both short sides of the remaining drawstring panel.

What You Need

Standard pillowcase with a 3½- to 4-inch-deep (8.9 to 10.2 cm) hem and only one side seam

1 yard (0.9 m) of clear iron-on vinyl for laminating fabric

Heavyweight/denim (size 14) sewing machine needle

Thread: white and to match the pillowcase and rickrack

2 yards (1.8 m) of rickrack, ¼ inch (0.6 cm) wide

1 yard (0.9 m) of white cotton twill tape, ½ inch (1.3 cm) wide

15 x 20-inch (38.1 x 50.8 cm) piece of fusible fleece

Skein of embroidery floss to match the pillowcase

Cellophane tape

Safety pin

1 yard (0.9 m) of cotton cord, ⅜ inch (9.5 mm) wide

1 yard (0.9 m) of lightweight fusible interfacing

SEAM ALLOWANCE

½ inch (1.3 cm) unless noted otherwise

Mix and Match

boxed lunch need not be a scruffy affair. Even if you're munching at your desk, you can treat yourself to an elegant meal by using a matching placemat. Simply reinforce the wrong side of each piece with interfacing so the placemat will last a long time. Use two 13 x 10-inch (33 x 25.4 cm) pieces for the placemat and a 3½ x 4 ½-inch (8.9 x 11.4 cm) piece to make the pocket.

This project won an online pillowcase challenge at www.handmadeparade.blogspot.com

6

Join the Panels

With the exterior panel face down, tape the ends of one of the handles, rickrack side down, on top of a short end of the panel. Each end of the handle should be 5 inches (12.7 cm) from the nearest side.

Sew one of the long edges of a drawstring panel, right side down, along this same edge. Remove the pieces of tape, cover the seam with the paper backing that you saved, and press the seam allowances and handle toward the exterior panel.

Topstitch on the exterior panel side of the seam line.

Attach the remaining handle and drawstring panel to the other side of the same exterior panel (see figure 1).

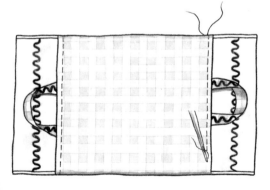

figure 1

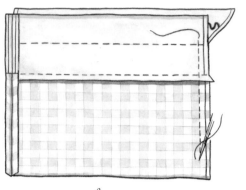

figure 2

7

Sew the Sides

Fold the joined panels in half with the right sides together and the seam lines and unattached long edges of the drawstring panels matching. Pin along both sides.

Starting 2 inches (5.1 cm) below the top of the drawstring panels, sew to the fold at the bottom. It's most important that you backstitch (see page 22) at both ends of the seam line.

Snip through the seam allowance at each fold line up to, but not through, the stitching and then press the seam allowances open (see figure 2).

8

Create the Drawstring Casing

Make a casing (see page 25) at the top of the drawstring panels by making two ½-inch-wide (1.3 cm) folds.

9

Set the Corners

Fold and flatten one of the corners at the bottom of the bag by matching a side seam to the fold line along the exterior panel. Sew across the corner, 2½ inches (6.4 cm) from the point. Repeat this step at the other corner.

10

Make the Lining

Iron fusible fleece to the wrong side of the lining panel, and create a 1½-inch (3.8 cm) diamond pattern or free-motion quilt as desired (see page 22).

Fold the panel in half with the right sides of the short ends matching. Sew the matched ends together. Box both corners the same way you did with the outside of the bag.

Fold under and topstitch the top raw edge.

11

Finish the Bag

Line up the bottoms of the exterior bag and lining, both wrong sides out. To strengthen the corners, use hand blanket stitches to sew together the corner seam allowances with embroidery floss (see figure 3).

Turn the bag right side out and hand stitch the lining to the side seams. Use the safety pin to thread the cotton cord through the top.

The vinyl coating on the outside of the bag will probably look pretty beat up. Use the paper backing you've set aside to press out any nicks and wrinkles.

12

Add a Flower Embellishment

Collect the pillowcase scraps and make your own flower (see Make the Flower on page 77) or pin a pre-made flower or other crafty item to your finished lunch box.

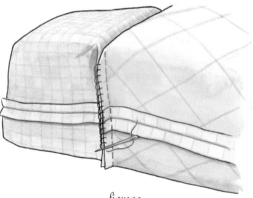

figure 3

sticker shock

Surprised by the way that vinyl clings to the sewing machine when you're trying to sew it? Switch to a Teflon presser foot for instant relief. If you have trouble sewing the vinyl with your standard foot and don't want to invest in a new presser foot, try placing a strip of tissue paper between your presser foot and the vinyl surface. The tissue can be ripped away when you're finished. (You might have to use tweezers to pull out the paper bits trapped in the stitching.)

Reversible Sun Hat

Kiss your parasol goodbye and say hello to twice the summer fashion.

Designed by Regina Lord

What You Need

2 standard pillowcases:
solid color and
complementary print

Tape measure

1 yard (0.9 m) of heavyweight,
iron-on interfacing

Thread to match
the pillowcases

SEAM ALLOWANCE
⅜ inch (9.5 mm)
unless noted otherwise

Project Instructions

1

Pick Your Size

Place a measuring tape around your head just at the top of your ears and across the middle of your forehead. Hold the tape firm but not too tight. Pick the appropriate hat size (see page 128). If your head measurement straddles two sizes, adjust the templates for a personal fit or choose one based on whether you want your hat snug or loose.

2

Make the Templates

Enlarge the crown, band, and brim patterns (see page 128). Copy the patterns to make templates.

3

Prepare the Fabric Shapes

Cut off the pillowcase hem and the seam at the closed end, keeping the sides intact. Refold the pillowcase so that the seam line is on the top layer and the crease from the fold line is on the bottom layer. Cut the fabric shapes from the pillowcase tube (see figure 1).

Fuse the interfacing shapes to the wrong sides of the two brim fabric pieces.

4

Join the Solid-Colored Band and Brim

Sew the two bands, right sides together, at both short ends to make a tube. These seam lines are the sides of the hat.

Pin—and then sew—the band to the crown with the right sides together, matching the notches and seam lines. Clip along the seam allowances (see page 24).

Sew the short ends of the brim together with the right sides facing. This seam line is the back of the hat.

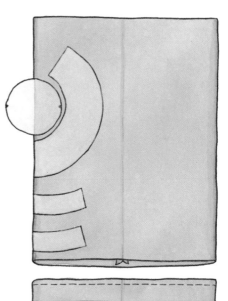

figure 1

Complete the Solid Hat

Sew the brim to the band with the right sides together, matching the brim seam line to a band notch and the remaining brim notch to a band notch.

Assemble the Printed Hat

Follow steps 1 through 5 to assemble the printed-fabric band, brim, and crown.

Join the Solid and Printed Hat

Tuck the solid-colored hat shape inside the printed shape with the right sides together (see figure 2). Sew around the matched brim edges, leaving a 4-inch (10.2 cm) opening at the back (see figure 2 again). Clip along the seam allowances (see page 24).

Press open the seam allowances all around the edge of both sides of the brim, including along the opening.

Turn the hat right side out through the opening. Sew the opening closed.

Add the Finishing Touches

Topstitch around the brim, ½ inch (1.3 cm) from the edge. Sew as many additional rows of topstitching as desired, placing the lines of stitching ½ inch (1.3 cm) apart.

figure 2

cupcake cuffs

These delicious little morsels are the stuff of dreams!

Pick out your favorite embellishments for a look that really pops.

Designed by Angela Cass

Project Instructions

───────────⬤①───────────

Make a Sandwich

Cut two 2¼ x 9-inch (5.7 x 22.9 cm) pieces from the pillowcase. Place them together with the wrong sides out. Place the fabric pieces between the two pieces of stabilizer.

Sew around the perimeter, rounding the corners and leaving a small opening. Clip the rounded corners (see page 24).

───────────⬤②───────────

Finish the Body

Turn the cuff right side out and push out the corners. You might want to use a point turner if you're having trouble with the corners. Top-stitch the perimeter.

Attach the snap parts—or add a button and buttonhole—near the ends.

───────────⬤③───────────

Add a Yo-Yo

Cut the fabric scrap to make a 3-inch-wide (7.6 cm) circle. Place the cardstock circle on the wrong side of the fabric circle. Thread a needle with a knotted length of the thread. Sew long running stitches around the perimeter of the fabric circle.

Pull the thread tight, so the fabric is taut around the cardstock. Tie off the thread, and remove the cardstock template.

Hand sew the yo-yo to the outside of the cuff. Sew a button in the center.

What You Need

(to make one)

Twin pillowcase

2 pieces of sew-in stabilizer, each 2¼ x 9 inches (5.7 x 22.9 cm)

Thread to match the pillowcase

Point turner (optional)

Snap or button, ⅜ inch (9.5 mm) wide

Fabric remnant, at least 3 inches (7.6 cm) square

Cardstock circle, 1½ inches (3.8 cm) in diameter

Decorative button, ½ inch (1.3 cm) in diameter

SEAM ALLOWANCE
¼ inch (6 mm)
unless noted otherwise

superhero cape

Faster than a speeding bullet—a two-sided cape zooms your little hero into action!

Designed by Stacy Dinkle

What You Need

King-size satin pillowcase

8-inch (20.3 cm) squares
of fabric remnants in four colors

Fray retardant

1⅔ yards (1.5 m)
of single-fold bias tape,
¼ inch (0.6 cm) wide

Thread to match
the pillowcase

Safety pin

25 inches (63.5 cm) of ribbon,
1 inch (2.5 cm) wide

SEAM ALLOWANCE
⅝ inch (15 mm)
unless noted otherwise

Project Instructions

1

Assemble the Superhero Patches

Enlarge the star and lightning bolt patterns on page 126, and make templates. Cut one of each from the fabric remnants, and apply fray blocker to the raw edges.

Cut two 8-inch-wide (20.3 cm) circles from the remaining remnants. Sew the symbols to the circles with machine straight stitches. Finish the circle edges by encasing them in the single-fold bias tape (see page 26).

2

Cut the Pillowcase

Measure your superhero child for the desired length. Measure from the open (hemmed) end of the pillowcase to the correct length, add 2 inches (5.1 cm), and cut across the entire width. The hemmed edge will be the bottom of the cape.

Cut open the pillowcase along the side that doesn't have a seam.

3

Attach the Symbols

Pin a symbol to the front of each half of the pillowcase. Sew them both in place using the stitching that attached the bias tape to the circles as a guide.

4

Join the Layers

Fold the pillowcase along the seam line (back into its original shape) with the wrong sides out. Join the two layers by sewing along the matched edges of the sides and bottom. Turn the cape right side out, and topstitch the sides and bottom.

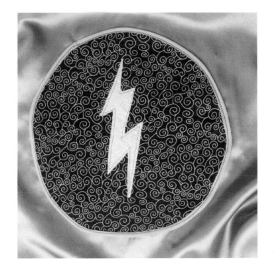

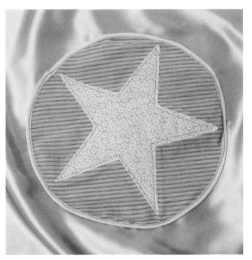

---
(5)

Finish the Neckline

Baste the top, raw edges together to close the top. Make a casing (see page 25) with a first fold that's ½ inch (1.3 cm) deep and a 1-inch-deep (2.5 cm) second fold.

Attach the safety pin to the ribbon, and pull it through the casing.

---
(6)

Custom Fit the Cape

Try the cape on your superhero and shift the gathers until 10 inches (25.4 cm) of ribbon extends out both ends of the casing. Adjust the lengths and the cape fit.

Separately sew across both ends of the casing through all of the layers to prevent the gathers from slipping along the exposed ribbon ties.

Getting a Grip

Here are a couple of suggestions to help you keep slippery satin under control when you're sewing.

- Set the machine for a smaller stitch length than usual.

- Move the needle to the far left (if your machine has this option) so more of the fabric is underneath the presser foot, which prevents it from shifting as much while you stitch.

- Sew plain, straight-stitch seams.

cuddle creature

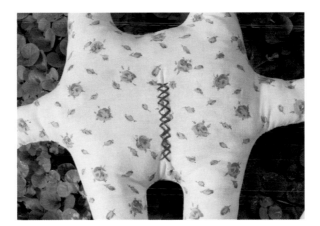

Make a new friend that's cute as a button, with personality to spare.

Designed by Mary Ann Abbott

What You Need

100-percent cotton,
standard pillowcase

2 vintage buttons,
1½ inches (3.8 cm) in diameter

Embroidery needle

Skein of coordinating embroidery floss

Thread to match the pillowcase

Polyester fiberfill

Fray retardant

Pinking shears

Safety pin

SEAM ALLOWANCE
½ inch (6 mm) unless noted otherwise

Project Instructions

Cut the Pillowcase

Enlarge the creature body pattern on page 126, and make a template. Lay the pillowcase flat so that it's two layers thick, and cut out the Body near the closed end of the pillowcase. Save the rest of the pillowcase for the gift bag (see page 95).

(2)

Add the Eyes

Pick one body piece for the front of the monster. On the right side of this piece, sew on the two button eyes using six strands of the embroidery floss. Position the eyes 2½ inches (6.4 cm) below the ears. Place them wide and high or narrow and low; the choice is yours.

(3)

Embroider the Face

Using six strands of thread, back stitch a straight line (see page 22) from the outer edge of the left eye to the outer edge of the right eye to make the mouth 1 inch (2.5 cm) below the eyes.

Add teeth using satin stitches (see page 21). The length and width of the teeth are for you to decide. The creature in the photos has a tooth under the third stitch from each end of the mouth.

Make a small satin-stitched heart—or another shape such as a starburst, "x," or dot—on the right ear.

Slit the Back Piece

Cut a 2½-inch (6.4 cm) vertical slit in the middle of the back piece, ending the slit ¾ inch (1.9 cm) from the bottom raw edge.

Fold under ¼ inch (0.6 cm) along both sides of the slit.

Machine stitch around the edge of the slit to control fraying.

(5)

Sew and Fill the Body

Place the front and back body pieces together with the right sides facing and the raw edges matching. Sew around the entire shape.

Turn the body right side out through the slit in the back piece.

Fill the monster with the polyester fiberfill by inserting it through the slit. Carefully stuff the corners to avoid splitting the seam. The squish factor is up to you; add as much of the fiberfill as you'd like.

Embroider the Details

At 1½ inches (3.8 cm) up from the bottom front, make one cross stitch (see page 21), working the floss through the back slit and the fiberfill. Pull the floss taut for a puckered belly button.

Using six strands of floss, embroider cross stitches along the back slit to close it. You can apply a bead of the fray retardant to the finished seam to help avoid fraying.

Gift Bag Instructions

---
(1)

Cut and Seam the Pieces

Cut two 14 x 17-inch (35.6 x 43.2 cm) pieces from the remaining pillowcase.

With the right sides together, sew the pieces together along both long sides and a short side.

Turn the joined pieces right side out. Trim the raw edge of the open end with the pinking shears.

---
(2)

Pack the Creature

Insert your little creature, fold over the flap, and close the bag with a safety pin.

... Live

springtime Bouquet

Patchwork coasters do more than just protect your table surface
from icy glassware—they look good doing it!

Designed by Katie Trott

Project Instructions

1
Cut the Materials

Make a 5-inch (12.7 cm) square template from the paper.

Use the template to cut four pieces from the interfacing and cut four backing pieces from one of the pillowcases.

2
Prepare the Tops

Cut five 8-inch (20.3 cm) long strips of fabric from each of the pillowcases to miscellaneous widths of 1, 2, and 3 inches (2.5, 5.1, and 7.6 cm) for each coaster.

Join the long sides of the strips together to make four pieced fabric rectangles, each one larger than the template. Press open the seam allowances after you make each seam.

Place the coaster template at a slight angle on top of each pieced rectangle and cut out the square shape.

3
Join the Layers

Make a sandwich for each coaster: interfacing on the bottom, a backing face up, and a pieced square right side down.

Sew around the perimeter of each sandwich, leaving a 2-inch (5.1 cm) long opening.

Clip the corners (see page 24) and turn the coasters right sides out.

Pin the opening closed and topstitch around the perimeter of each coaster.

What You Need

(to make four coasters)

5 standard pillowcases

10-inch (25.4 cm) square
of medium-weight sew-in interfacing

Pencil

Sheet of paper

Thread to match the pillowcase

SEAM ALLOWANCE

¼ inch (6 mm)
unless noted otherwise

Dream catcher

Crochet a knotted bowl with pillowcase strips!

Designed by Jennifer Thoma

What you need

Standard pillowcase

Crochet hook
size K/10.5 (7 mm)

Stitch marker
that opens and closes

Large tapestry (or yarn) needle
with a blunt point

- - - - - - - - - -

ABBREVIATIONS

ch chain

inc Increase

pm place marker

rep repeat

rnd round(s)

sc single crochet

sl st(s) slip stitch(es)

st(s) stitch(es)

Project Instructions

---
(1)

Cut the Pillowcase

Cut off and discard the hem, the seam at the closed end, and the side seams. Spread the pillowcase flat by opening it along the fold.

Starting at the bottom on one side, cut ¾-inch (1.9 cm) wide strips by cutting across the width, pivoting without cutting through the raw edge at the opposite side, and then cutting in the opposite direction across the width. Continue until you've cut the entire pillowcase into one long piece.

---
(2)

Start a Circle

Make a slip knot at an end of the fabric strip and slide it onto the crochet hook. Ch 6 (see figure 1). Sl st in first ch to form a circle (see figure 2). Ch 1.

---
(3)

Make the Base

Rnd 1: 12 sc in circle (see figure 3), pm. [12 sc] Notes: Work all sc in both top loops of previous sc for all rnds. Move marker to last st of every rnd.

Rnd 2: Sc in each sc around.

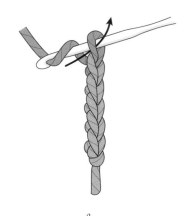

figure 1

figure 2

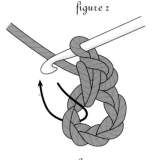

figure 3

4

Work Increases for the Side

Rnd 3 (Inc): 2 sc in each st around. [24 sc]

Rnd 4: Sc in each sc around.

Rnd 5 (Inc): *Sc in next sc, 2 sc in next sc, rep from * around. [36 sc]

Rnd 6: Sc in each sc around.

5

Complete the Side

Rep Rnd 6 for 3 more times or until the fabric strip is 6 inches (15.2 cm) long. Fasten off. Use the tapestry needle to weave the fabric end through the completed stitches.

Color Fast

Introduce a stripe in any round with a fabric strip cut from a second, complementary pillowcase. Change to the new strip with the first loop (yarn over hook) you make during a single crochet. Leave a 3-inch (7.6 cm) end hanging loose, to weave in when the bowl is complete.

Think Big

You can make a large bowl just as easily as a small one. Cut strips from four pillowcases, and make the small bowl to the end of step 4. Now work even (no increases) for the next two rounds. Increase for the sides by working two single crochet in every third stitch of the next round. Now you have 48 stitches. Continue increasing 12 stitches every third row. When the bowl is the desired size, fasten off.

Decorative Box

An up-cycled cigar box covered in harmonizing pillowcases is the perfect place to store recipes, craft supplies, or love letters.

Designed by Katie Trott

Project Instructions

Make the Templates

Open the box lid and trace the perimeter on the paper. (Close the lid to trace the next side.) Trace the box bottom.

Remove the box and draw cutting lines ½ inch (1.3 cm) beyond the originals to make the lid and bottom templates.

Cut the last two sheets of paper in half lengthwise, and tape them together end to end. Create a side template by tracing the box's sides as one continuous rectangle onto the paper. Add 1 inch (2.5 cm) to the width and length of the traced shape.

Cut the paper along the outer lines.

Cut the Pillowcases

Cut off the hem, the seam at the closed end, and one side of both pillowcases.

Use the Lid template to cut two pieces (for the inner and outer lids) from the printed pillowcase.

Cut two sides and two bottoms from the solid-colored pillowcase.

③ Cover the Outer Lid

Test the fit of the outer lid piece on the top of the box. (In fact, test-fit all of the pieces before you permanently attach them to the box.) Coat the box lid with the fabric spray adhesive. Press on the printed fabric outer lid, smoothing it to eliminate wrinkles and bubbles. Make sure that the lid still opens easily. Miter the corners, then apply spray to the lid edges and the interior of the sides, and press the excess fabric to the inside. Any spray that lands on the fabric won't be visible or tacky when dry.

④ Cover the Exterior Sides

Beginning at the middle back of the box, wrap the exterior sides to make sure the side piece fits and the short ends overlap. Apply adhesive to the box, and press on the fabric so the long edges extend beyond the top and bottom of the box and the short ends overlap, folding under the short end that's on top for a clean, finished seam.

Apply adhesive to the inside of the box, and then attach the top edge of the side piece to the inside the box. Apply adhesive to the box bottom, and then attach the bottom edge of the side piece to bottom of the box.

What You Need

2 standard pillowcases:
print and coordinating solid

Cigar box,
5 x 8½ x 2⅜ inches
(12.7 x 21.6 x 1 cm)

3 sheets of paper,
each 8½ x 11 inches
(21. 6 x 27.9 cm)

Pencil

Fabric spray adhesive

30 inches (76 cm)
of coordinating decorative ribbon,
1½ inches (3.8 cm) wide

Pinking shears
(optional)

Roll of decorative craft tape,
1½ inches (3.8 cm) wide

5

Attach a Ribbon

Cut the ribbon into two 15-inch (38.1 cm) lengths. Set one length aside. Glue one end of the remaining length to the center of the lid's interior.

6

Attach the Inner Lid

Press under ½ inch (1.3 cm) on all sides of the inner lid (or cut off this amount using the pinking shears). Adhere the inner lid to the box, covering the exposed ribbon edge.

7

Finish the Interior

Fold under the long ends and one short end of the remaining fabric piece. Adjust the folds to fit along the sides of the box's interior, leaving the top edge folded under and the bottom edge folded up. Glue the piece in place.

8

Add Another Ribbon Length

Glue the short end of the other piece of ribbon to the bottom of the box at the center front.

9

Add the Bottom

Fold under (or pink) the edges of both bottoms so that one piece fits the underside of the box and the other fits inside the box. Glue them in place.

10

Tape the Inner Hinge

Apply a piece of the decorative craft tape along the length of the hinge inside the box.

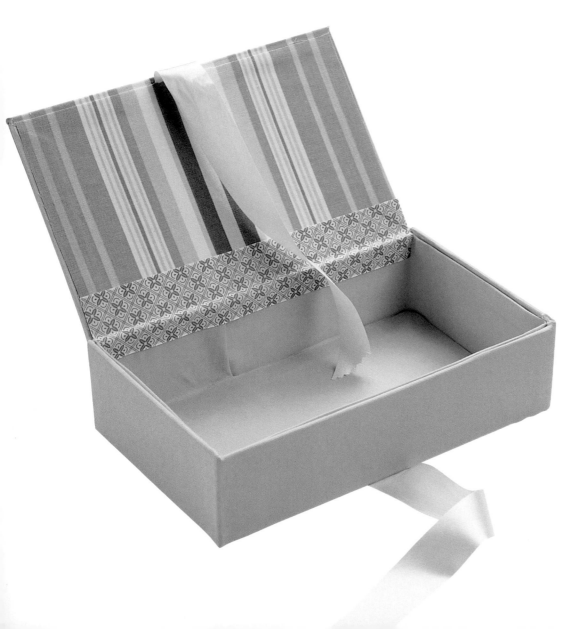

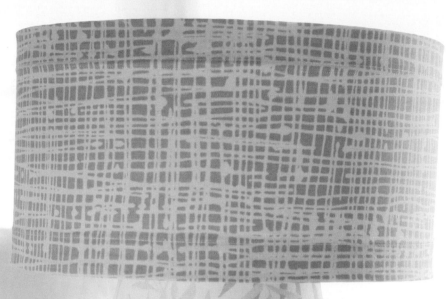

Eco Deco

Make your favorite pillowcases shine! Things are always cooler in the shade, and this lampshade's got coolness covered.

Designed by Joan K. Morris

What you need

Standard pillowcase
with print

King-size pillowcase
with complementary print

8-inch-tall (20.3 cm) coolie
(cylinder with flared base)
lampshade, 5 inches
(12.7 cm) diameter

Pen

2 pieces of paper,
each 25 inches (63.5 cm) square

6-inch-tall (15.2 cm)
shallow drum lampshade,
11 inches (27.9 cm) diameter

Thread to match

Small hole punch

18 inches (61 cm)
of 24-gauge wire

Wire cutters

SEAM ALLOWANCE

½ inch (1.3 cm)
unless noted otherwise

Project Instructions

1

Make the Coolie Template

Roll the coolie lampshade—starting at the vertical seam—while using the pen to trace the top and bottom edges onto the paper. Cut out the shape, and wrap it around the coolie shade to check the fit.

Trace the shape a second time onto your second piece of paper. Add 1 inch (2.5 cm) along the entire bottom edge, ¼ inch (0.6 cm) to the upper edge, and ½ inch (1.3 cm) to both side ends. Cut this out for your coolie template.

2

Cut the Fabric Shapes

Cut off and discard the hem and the seams at the closed end and one side of both pillowcases. Open them flat, and use the coolie template to cut the shape from the standard pillowcase.

From the king-size pillowcase, cut out a rectangle that's 2 inches (5.1 cm) longer than the drum shade's circumference and 2½ inches (6.4 cm) taller than the height.

3

Hem the Edges

Narrow hem the upper edge of the coolie fabric shape using ¼-inch-deep (0.6 mm) folds.

Hem the drum fabric piece by folding under ¼ inch (0.6 cm) and then 1 inch (2.5 cm) along each long side.

4

Fit the Fabric Piece

Place each fabric piece wrong side out in position on the corresponding lampshade. Pin the matched ends together so that the fabric fits tightly.

Remove the fabric from the shade, and machine stitch along the pinned line.

Finish the raw edges of the short ends by sewing together the seam allowances with zigzag stitching as close as you can to the seam line you just made. Cut off the excess fabric beyond the zigzag stitching, and press the seam allowances to one side. Turn the fabric right side out, and topstitch with straight stitching close to the seam.

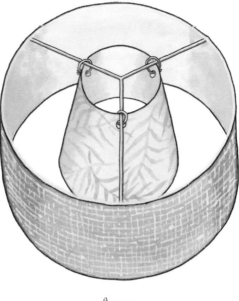

figure 1

5

Complete the Coolie Cover

Place the sewn piece for the coolie shade wrong side out on the lampshade. Fold up and pin the bottom of the fabric to align with the bottom of the shade.

Take the fabric piece off the shade, press the fold, and remove the pins. Tuck the raw edge inside the folded edge, and sew this doubled hem. Turn the piece right side out.

6

Complete the Shades

Slide the pieces over the corresponding shades.

7

Align the Shades

Place the shades together, lining up the seams at the back. Pen-mark the top of the coolie shade where the drum shade's wires cross. Separate the shades and remove the fabric cover on the smaller shade. Punch holes in the smaller shade just under the top ring, at the marked positions.

8

Connect the Shades

Cut three 6-inch (15.2 cm) pieces of the wire. Align the metal support bars in both shades with the coolie shade beneath the drum shade. Wrap the wire through the punched hole and around the aligned support bars, creating a knotted loop (see figure 1). Repeat this step with the other two holes, and cut off any excess wire.

Fit to Be Tied

The key to success is finding two lamp-shades that look attractive when stacked. Don't be afraid to play around with the shapes at the stores. The lampshades used for the finished project (page 107) were found at a craft store and a secondhand store.

Flower Bed

Pamper your pet with a dreamy place to rest made from contrasting pillowcase patterns.

Designed by Eren Hays San Pedro

Project Instructions

1

Cut the Pillowcases

Cut off the seam at the closed end and along one side of both pillowcases. Rip out the hem stitching, and unfold the hem allowance.

Both open pillowcases must be at least 35 x 44 inches (88.9 x 111.8 cm).

2

Seam the Zipper Edge

Place the pillowcases with right sides facing, and baste them together along one long side with a ¼ inch (6 mm) seam allowance.

Measure off 35 inches (88.9 cm) along the center of the basted line, and pin-mark the beginning and end.

Sew regular-length straight stitch seam lines on top of the basting from the raw edges to the pins, but don't seam the central 35 inches (88.9 cm).

3

Insert the Zipper

Press open the seam allowances. Pull out the basting so you have a long opening in the joined pieces.

Pin the closed zipper between the two pressed edges, both right side up. Let the bottom of the zipper extend beyond the opening. The loose end of the zipper tape can remain inside the finished cover.

Sew one side of the tape in place a bit more than ⅛ inch (3 mm) from a folded edge. Sew straight across the zipper at the bottom of the opening and then back up the other folded side (see figure 1).

4

Join the Rectangles

Fold the two pieces of fabric along the zipper with the right sides together. Pin the rest of the fabric edges together. Trim any extra material to make both rectangles the same size. Open the zipper.

Sew the rectangles together.

Turn the cover right side out and insert the dog bed.

figure 1

What You Need

2 king pillowcases:
complementary prints

Thread to match
the pillowcases

36-inch-long
(76.2 cm) zipper

Zipper presser foot
(optional but highly recommended)

26 x 35 x 7-inch
(66 x 89 x 17.8 cm) dog bed

SEAM ALLOWANCE

½ inch (13 cm)
unless noted otherwise

haute pad

Too hot to handle?
Not with this mitt.
Felt appliqués add some
sizzle, and interior
batting keeps things cool.

Designed by Nathalie Mornu

Project Instructions

---
①

Cut the Pattern Pieces

Photocopy the appliqué design pieces on page 127. Use these templates to cut out the felt shapes.

Cut two 10-inch (25.4 cm) squares from the pillowcase and two from the silver cloth. Place one of the pillowcase squares face up on the ironing board, and arrange all the felt pieces on it—as shown in the photo—matching the straight edges of the felt with the edges of the pillowcase square.

---
②

Attach the Appliqués

Tack down the felt pieces with little bits of the fusible web pressed with a hot iron.

Pin the right side of one of the silver squares to the wrong side of this pillowcase square. Machine topstitch around the edges of the felt appliqués except for the circular shapes. Hand stitch around them with fairly large stitches. Set this back aside.

---
③

Prepare the Other Pieces

Pin the right side of the remaining silver square to the wrong side of the remaining pillowcase square, and baste around the edges. Set this front aside.

---
④

Make a Hanging Tab

Cut a 1½ x 8-inch (3.8 x 20.3 cm) strip from the pillowcase. Press it in half lengthwise. Open it, and fold the long raw edges in to meet the crease. Sew the long folded edges together.

---
⑤

Make a Sandwich

Cut a 9-inch (22.9 cm) square from the batting. Stack the layers as follows: stabilizer on the bottom, batting, back right side up, and front wrong side up. Tuck the tab into a corner between the front and back, making sure the loop faces toward the center of the squares and the batting is centered beneath the squares.

Stitch around the perimeter, leaving a 6-inch (15.2 cm) opening and catching the edges of the batting in the stitching. Tear away the stabilizer, clip the corners, and turn the layers right side out.

Pin the opening shut and topstitch around the entire perimeter.

What You Need

100-percent cotton pillowcase, any size

⅛ yard (0.1 m) of high-quality wool felt in two colors

⅜ yard (0.34 m) of heat-resistant silver cloth

6-inch (15.2 cm) square of fusible web

Thread to match the felt

¼ yard (0.3 m) of cotton batting

10-inch square (25.4 cm) of tear-away stabilizer

SEAM ALLOWANCE

½ inch (1.3 cm) unless noted otherwise

Oh, Baby! Quilt

You don't have to be a tot to appreciate this soft and simple baby quilt
—easy hand-tied patchwork wraps you in pillowcase bliss.

Designed by Eren Hays San Pedro

What you need

Four standard pillowcases:
3 coordinating
and 1 contrasting print

Thread to match
the pillowcases

Flat twin bedsheet to coordinate
with the pillowcases

Quilt batting, content and
thickness as desired

Skein of cotton
medium-weight yarn
or embroidery floss to contrast
the pillowcases

SEAM ALLOWANCE

¼ inch (6 mm)
unless noted otherwise

- - - - - - - - - - - - - - - -

NOTES

Throughout these steps refer
to the whole quilt template
and always press
the seam allowances toward
the darker fabric
when joining the pieces.

Project Instructions

Make the Rectangles

For each pillowcase, cut off the seams at the closed end and one side, and then cut along the vertical fold. Rip out the hem stitching. You now have eight rectangles: two each of A, B, C, and D.

Tweak the Shapes

Cut the rectangles so they're the same size and the length of each one is 1½ times its width. For example, if the length is 32 inches (81.3 cm), then cut the width to 21⅓ inches (54.2 cm): $32 \div 1½ = 21⅓$.

Join the Pieces

Cut a B rectangle in half lengthwise. Sew a C to a halved B along one long edge with the right sides facing. Join the remaining C to the other halved B.

Sew the lengthwise edge of an A to a B/C set with the right sides facing. Join the remaining A to the other B/C set.

Finish the Quilt Top

Rotate the A/B/C rectangles so that an A is at the top of one set and at the bottom of the other. Sew the sets together along one long edge with the right sides facing.

Join the Quilt Layers

Prepare the backing by cutting the bedsheet to 2 inches (5.1 cm) longer and wider than the quilt top. Cut the batting to the same size as the backing.

Stack the backing right side down, the batting, and the quilt top right side up.

Starting at the center and working outward in a spiral, pin or baste the layers together every 5 inches (12.7 cm).

---

(6)

Tie the Layers

Thread the yarn or six strands of embroidery floss onto a needle with a sharp point, and draw it through the layers starting at the center of the quilt top and ending on the underside. Pull the yarn or floss up to the front ¼ inch (0.6 cm) from the original insertion point. Knot the ends, and cut them to 1 inch (2.5 cm) long. Continue making ties every 6 inches (15.2 cm) over the entire quilt.

(7)

Bind the Quilt

Cut the remaining two D rectangles into 1-inch-wide (2.5 cm) strips. Piece and sew these end to end to make a length that will go around the entire quilt. Bind the edges of the quilt (see page 26), folding the binding to form a 45° angle at each corner.

under control

Keep all those remote controls in an elegant organizer — instead of the seat cushions.

Designed by Jeanette Reichard

Project Instructions

1
Cut the Pieces

Cut off and discard the hem, one side seam, and the seam at the closed end of the pillowcase. Open it flat, and cut out the fabric shapes: two 12½ x 10-inch (31.8 x 25.4 cm) pieces for the front and back and one 12½ x 6½-inch (31.8 x 16.5 cm) piece for the pocket.

2
Attach the Pocket

Narrow hem one long edge of the pocket.

Baste together the matched raw edges of the pocket and the front with both right side up.

3
Add the Ties

Cut the ribbon in half to make two 1-yard (0.9 m) lengths. Fold each one in half across the width. Baste the folded edge of each ribbon at the top of the front (see figure 1).

figure 1

4
Make a Sandwich

Stack the pieces as follows: interfacing, the front/pocket right side up, and the back right side down. Sew around the edges through all of the layers.

5
Topstitch the Layers

Topstitch around the outer edges and then vertically through the pocket to make three separate sections (see figure 2).

figure 2

What You Need

Standard pillowcase

Thread to match the pillowcase

2 yards (1.8 m) of ribbon, 1½ inches (3.8 cm) wide

12½ x 10 inches (31.8 x 25.4 cm) of heavyweight sew-in interfacing

SEAM ALLOWANCE

¼ inch (6 mm) unless noted otherwise

Tea Time

Cozy up your teapot with some piping hot tea, and take a little break from the world.

Designed by Judi Music

Project Instructions

① Cut the Pillowcase

Cut off and discard the hem, the seam at the closed end, and the side seam. Spread the pillowcase flat by opening it along the fold.

Enlarge the pattern on page 126 to make a template. Cut out the shapes as noted.

Cut a 2 x 23-inch (5.1 x 58.4 cm) solid-color strip from the pillowcase.

② Prepare the Ruffle

Fold the fabric strip in half lengthwise. Handling the two raw edges as one, baste the edge and pull the top thread to make the ruffle.

③ Attach the Ruffle

Make a sandwich in the following order: lining piece right side down, batting (or flannel), pillowcase piece right side up, and ruffle with the folded edge to the inside. Baste the layers together around all of the edges except the straight bottom.

④ Add the Other Layers

Align the raw edges of all the layers in the following order: previously joined layers with the ruffle on top, pillowcase piece right side down, batting (or flannel), and the last lining piece right side up.

Sew the layers together around all sides except the bottom. Overcast or zigzag stitch the seam allowances together.

Turn the tea cozy right side out so the folded ruffle edge is exposed and the raw edges are hidden. Bind the bottom raw edges (see page 26).

see page 26

What You Need

Standard cotton pillowcase*

½ yard (0.5 m)
of complementary cotton fabric
for the lining, 44 inches (115 cm) wide

14-inch (35.6 cm) square
of batting (any type) or flannel

Thread to complement
the pillowcase

30 inches (76.2 cm)
of extra-wide double-fold bias tape

* If the pillowcase doesn't
have a solid-color section,
you also need a 2 x 23-inch
(5.1 x 58.4 cm) strip of solid-color fabric.

SEAM ALLOWANCE

½ inch (1.3 cm)
unless noted otherwise

Best Pressed

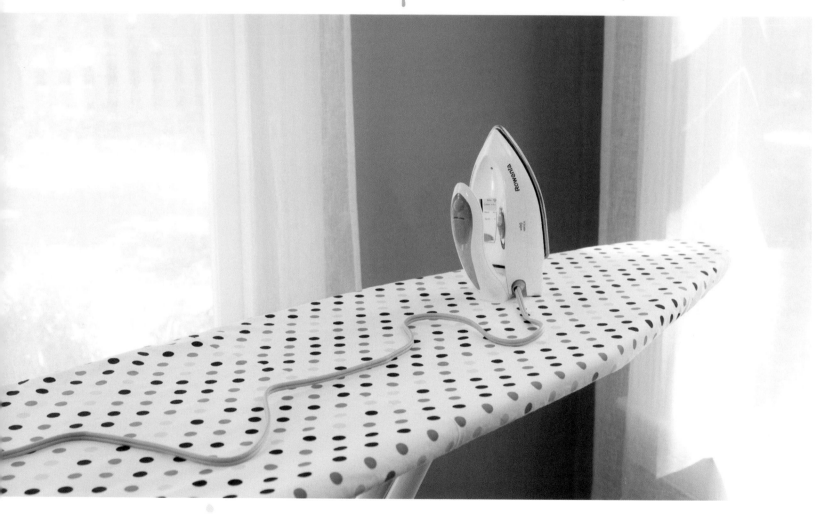

Ironing is never a bore with a cheerful cover-up for your board.

You'll be steamed you never thought of it before!

Designed by Joan K. Morris

Project Instructions

1

Prepare the Pillowcase

Cut off the side seam and the seam at the closed end of your pillowcase. Cut along the opposite side of the pillowcase, along the vertical fold. Rip out the hem stitching.

Join the pillowcase pieces at a short end to make one length. Finish the raw edges with zig-zag stitching along the seam allowances, and press the seams open.

2

Shape the Piece

Place the joined pillowcase pieces right side down on a flat work surface. Place the ironing board, with the old cover removed, upside down in the center of the fabric. (Save the old ironing board cover; you can use it as padding underneath the new cover.)

Trace around the ironing board 3 inches (7.6 cm) out from the edges. Cut out the shape along this line.

3

Finish the Perimeter

Make a casing (see page 25) with ¼- and ¾-inch-deep (0.6 and 1.9 cm) folds, leaving a 3-inch (7.6 cm) opening at the bottom, flat end. Before making the second fold, baste all of the curves. After removing the fabric from the sewing machine, pull the top (needle) thread until each curve is drawn in enough so the cover will lay flat.

4

Insert the Elastic

Place the safety pin at one end of the elastic, and run it through the casing. Draw up the ends of the elastic so that the cover is a tight fit on the ironing board top. Cut the elastic to length, butt the ends, and join them with several overlapping rows of zigzag stitching.

Sew the opening closed with appliqué stitches.

What You Need

Standard pillowcase*

Thread to match the pillowcase

Safety pin

3 yards (2.7 m) of elastic,
½ inch (1.3 cm) wide

*You'll need a second pillowcase
if the widest part of your
ironing board is greater than
14½ inches (36.8 cm).

SEAM ALLOWANCE

½ inch (1.3 cm)
unless noted otherwise

Just Ducky

Go ahead and stick it to this sweet guy (think of it as acupuncture).
The brown felt wings are for storing needles.

Designed by Cassi Griffin

Project Instructions

1

Cut the Pillowcase

Trace the patterns (see page 126) onto the freezer paper and cut them out. Turn the pillowcase inside out. Iron the freezer paper template for the body, shiny side down, to the top layer of the pillowcase. Pin around it, through both layers.

Sew through the pillowcase layers around the edge of the body template, leaving an opening as marked on the pattern. Pull off the template.

2

Make the Body

Cut out the body ¼ inch (0.6 cm) outside the stitching. Clip through the seam allowances at the curves (see page 24), and press open the seam allowances at the opening.

Turn the body right side out. Stuff it with polyester fiberfill and rice or lentils. Appliqué stitch the opening closed.

3

Build the Wings

Cut two wings from the cream wool felt. Cut two from the coordinating fabric using the pinking shears. Make sure the wings point in opposite directions when the fabric is right side up.

Topstitch a fabric wing to each felt wing using a ⅛-inch (3 mm) seam allowance.

Cut two wings from the brown wool felt ⅛ inch (3 mm) outside the pattern lines using the pinking or scalloping shears.

4

Attach the Wings

Use straight stitches to hand sew the front edge of the wing layers—with the brown felt on the bottom—to the body.

5

Make a Face

Sew on the buttons for eyes. Cut one beak from the yellow wool felt. Fold the piece in half, and sew it over the fabric body's beak with small stitches and two strands of the embroidery floss.

Hungry for more?
Find another bonus pincushion project at www.larkbooks.com/crafts.

What You Need

Standard pillowcase

Freezer paper

Thread to match the pillowcase

Polyester fiberfill

Rice or lentils

High-quality wool felt:
6-inch (15.2 cm) squares
of brown and cream,
2½ x 1½-inch
(6.4 x 3.8 cm) piece of yellow

5-inch (12.7 cm) square
of coordinating fabric

Pinking shears

Scalloping shears (optional)

2 buttons, ⅜ inch (9.5 mm) wide

12 inches (30.5 cm)
of embroidery floss
to match the yellow felt

SEAM ALLOWANCE

¼ inch (6 mm)
unless noted otherwise

Templates

ENLARGE 300%

ENLARGE 300%

ENLARGE 500%

ENLARGE 500%

ENLARGE 300%

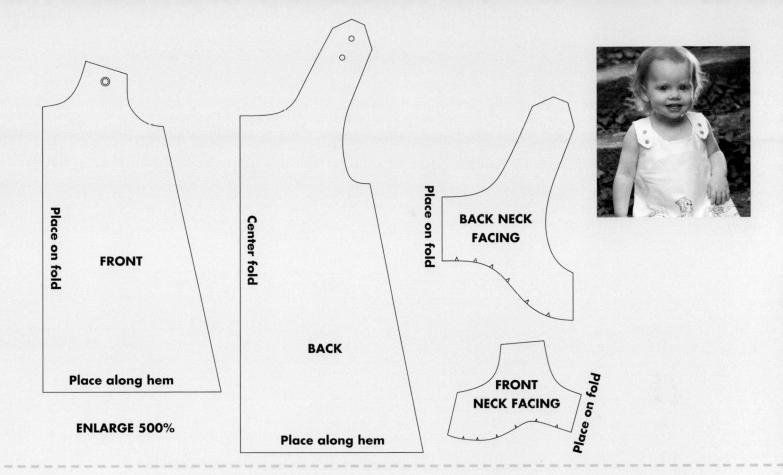

Place on fold

FRONT

Place along hem

ENLARGE 500%

Center fold

BACK

Place along hem

Place on fold

BACK NECK FACING

FRONT NECK FACING

Place on fold

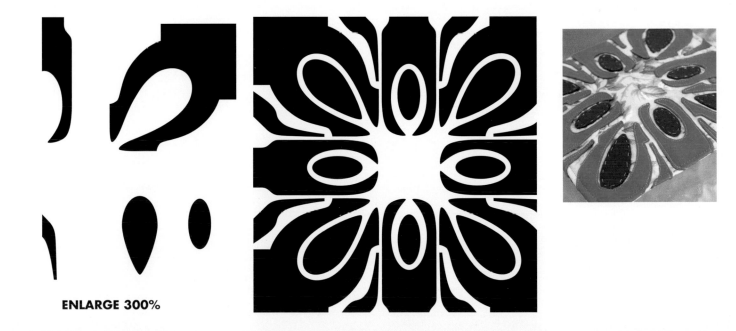

ENLARGE 300%

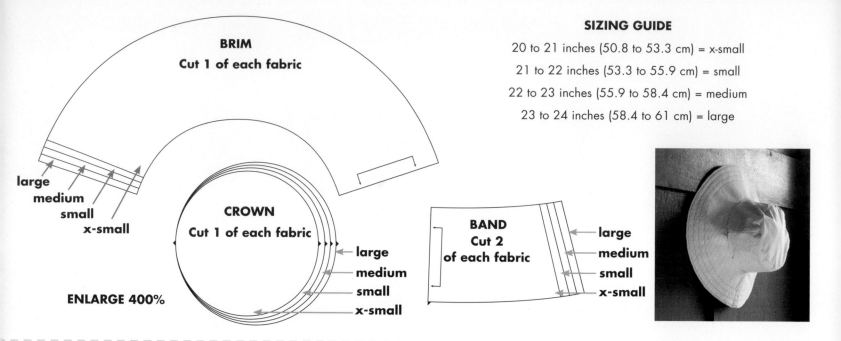

BRIM
Cut 1 of each fabric

large
medium
small
x-small

CROWN
Cut 1 of each fabric

large
medium
small
x-small

ENLARGE 400%

BAND
Cut 2
of each fabric

large
medium
small
x-small

SIZING GUIDE

20 to 21 inches (50.8 to 53.3 cm) = x-small

21 to 22 inches (53.3 to 55.9 cm) = small

22 to 23 inches (55.9 to 58.4 cm) = medium

23 to 24 inches (58.4 to 61 cm) = large

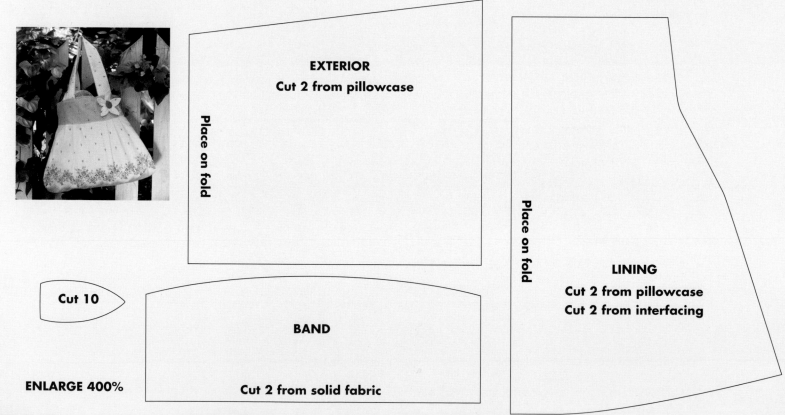

EXTERIOR
Cut 2 from pillowcase

Place on fold

Place on fold

LINING
Cut 2 from pillowcase
Cut 2 from interfacing

Cut 10

BAND
Cut 2 from solid fabric

ENLARGE 400%

Acknowledgments

A standing ovation is in order for the designers who created the book's clever, innovative, darling, and downright dreamy projects. We were forever amazed by the ways you thought "outside the pillowcase"—thank you!

As the adage goes, it takes a village to raise a child, and it took a very talented group of Larkers to bring this book together (a whole season early, I might add!). Thanks to Beth Sweet for curating a beautiful collection of projects and developmental details and to Nicole McConville, who jumped into the pillowcase rollercoaster and shared great vision at every turn. We couldn't have stayed on track without the finely tuned organizational prowess of Linda Kopp and the proofreading finesse of Amanda Carestio—merci.

Susan Huxley, the book's technical editor and Sewing Queen, contributed keen insight to every page, and Orrin Lundgren's gorgeous illustrations bring the written word to life.

Many thanks to art director Dana Irwin whose imagination brought stunning perspective and vitality to the book's design and personality. Junior designer Carol Morse is to be lauded for her beautiful page layout, and kudos go to Shannon Yokeley for her dedicated art assistance. Photographer Lynne Harty caught all the right light at all the right moments, even at sunrise on a mountaintop!

Many models shared their talent with us, including Lark's very own interns Katie Henderson, Meagan Shirlen, and Cynthia LeGrande. Sprinkled among the projects are some sweet pillowcase memories from Amanda Carestio, Mary Gaston, Heidi Grimshaw, Katy Hanson, and Jacqueline Wolven. The divine "stash" pillowcases were graciously loaned to us by Vanessa Greenhow, Emily Schildhouse, Terry Taylor, Jennie Thoma, Katie Trott, and Karrie Weaver. From start to finish, this has been one stellar challenge!

Designers

English professor by day and crafty chica by night, MARY ANN ABBOTT feels most at home in her attic studio where she has been creating her whimsical wares for over a decade. She feels passionate about words, vintage goodies, and repurposing unloved treasures from thrift shops, yard sales, and flea markets. Her artwork has been featured in *Somerset Studio* and *Flowers &*, and her freelance writing has appeared in multiple magazines, journals, and online venues. Mary Ann invites you to visit her at www.averymarydesign.com.

CARISSA ADAMS is a fledgling seamstress and a full-time creative artist. She currently splits her time between college courses, thrift shopping, and her creative endeavors. She is most often found in her private studio at her Florida home or on location passionately shooting photos. She is the founder and CEO of Chick Habit, her own label for handmade and vintage "remixed" clothing. You can find her on the web at www.ChickHabit.etsy.com.

Stitchy McYarnpants is the nom-de-plume of mild-mannered computer programmer DEBBIE BRISSON, a crafty gal with a penchant for all things vintage. Stitchy enjoys sewing from a vast stash of vintage fabrics. When yarn and fabric won't do, you can find her leafing through stacks of old magazines, clipping images to use for one-of-a-kind cards, key chains, and buttons that herald those long ago days of yesterweird. Check out her latest creations at her Etsy shop: www.McYarnpants.etsy.com

ANGELA CASS is a self-taught artist residing in San Antonio, Texas. Her work often incorporates the discarded items of everyday life, such as bed linens, rusted hardware, and old books. Angela's mediums of choice are sewing, assemblage art, and jewelry making. Her creations can be viewed online at www.airportroad.etsy.com, and you can email her at airport.road@yahoo.com.

STACY DINKEL, creator of the "Doodle Factory," is a stay-at-home mom, part-time social worker, and a woman with a lot of pent-up creativity. She has a bachelor's degree in Fine Arts and a master's degree in Counseling: both degrees have helped her hone her skills as an artist. Quite simply, she's never met an art or craft she doesn't like. Visit Stacy's Etsy shop at www.MamasDoodles.etsy.com, and read about her creative endeavors at http://mamasdoodles.blogspot.com.

LEE-ANN EDWARDS lives in Texas, but her love of sewing started as a young 4-H'er in the Midwest corn country of Indiana. With the arrival of her daughter in 2002, Lee-Ann created Whoopsie Daisies, a collection of items for you and your children made from previously loved vintage linens and materials. She believes in honoring the women from the past by using and loving their handmade creations, and she believes that each piece has a history and soul that deserves to be remembered. Visit her website and blog at www.whoopsiedaisies.etsy.com and www.whoopsiedaisiesdays.blogspot.com.

MELISSA FEHR grew up in Pennsylvania, but it wasn't until she moved to London in 2002 that she taught herself to sew using an old hand-me-down machine. Her recycled fabric dresses gained the attention of the fashion press and resulted in her work being featured in the *New York Times*, *Financial Times*, *Daily Express* (London), and *Elle* magazine. Melissa counts her studio as one of the few floating sewing workshops in the world—she lives on a large Dutch barge on the Thames in view of Tower Bridge. Visit Melissa's Fehr Trade label at www.fehrtrade.com.

VANESSA GREENHOW enjoys fabricating unique clothing and jewelry from vintage and upcycled supplies. She currently lives in beautiful British Columbia, Canada, with her supportive husband and two crafty kids. You can find more of her original creations at her website, timeoforiginshop.com, or follow her blog at http://timeoforigin.blogspot.com.

CASSI GRIFFIN is a craft designer residing in the mountains of Idaho with her three children and more than a dozen pets. In addition to running her home design and textile business, Cassi keeps busy as a single homeschooling mom and contributes to many craft books and national magazines. You can view Cassi's work at two blogs: Bella Dia (http://belladia.typepad.com), which features her work and tutorials, and The Crafty Crow (http://belladia.typepad.com/crafty_crow), a children's craft collective.

ELIZABETH HARTMAN is a self-taught sewer, pattern designer, and crafting enthusiast who has worked at a variety of day jobs including a plastic factory, making patches for high school letterman jackets, marketing and public relations for a fine arts organization, and closing loans on commercial real estate. More recently,